Penguin Special
The Property Machine

Peter Ambrose was born in 1933 and left school at
sixteen. Having spent eleven years working in a bank in
the City and serving in the R.A.F., he re-embarked on his
education, and graduated from King's College, London
with a B.A. (Hons.) and from McGill University,
Canada with an M.A. He also received a D.Phil from
Sussex University and has worked there since 1965,
currently as a lecturer in the School of Cultural and
Community Studies. He is also a tutor, consultant and
broadcaster for the Open University and has been
a visiting professor at McMaster, Trent and McGill
Universities in Canada.

Bob Colenutt was born in London in 1942. He went to
King's College, London, and graduated in the same year
as Peter Ambrose. He received an M.Sc. at Pennsylvania
State University and worked for a planning consultant
for a year. He then obtained a doctorate in geography
from Bristol University and returned to the U.S.A. to
teach urban geography at Syracuse University. During
this time he also worked with community groups in
Detroit. Since 1972, he has been full-time research
worker for the North Southwark Community
Development Group, a federation of local organizations
concerned with redevelopment in Southwark.

Peter Ambrose and Bob Colenutt

The Property Machine

Penguin Books

Penguin Books Ltd, Harmondsworth,
Middlesex, England
Penguin Books Inc., 7110 Ambassador Road,
Baltimore, Maryland 21207, U.S.A.
Penguin Books Australia Ltd, Ringwood,
Victoria, Australia
Penguin Books Canada Ltd, 41 Steelcase Road West,
Markham, Ontario, Canada
Penguin Books (N.Z.) Ltd, 182–190 Wairau Road,
Auckland 10, New Zealand

First published 1975

Copyright © Peter Ambrose and Bob Colenutt, 1975

Made and printed in Great Britain by
Hazell Watson & Viney Ltd,
Aylesbury, Bucks
Set in Linotype Plantin

To Liz

Contents

Urban redevelopment plays the part of a secondary process parallel to that of industrial production. It is a compensating process: when the surplus value created by industry sinks to a low level, surplus value created by construction and speculative development rises instead. Urban planning masks this relationship and in so doing prevents not only a clear understanding of urban phenomena, but also the proper *use* of the city itself. This is why planning must be subjected to a radical critique which in the end will refute the state, its strategies and its misuse of urban space.

Henri Lefebvre

Acknowledgements

Many people helped us in the preparation of this book. We would like to thank the following, some of whom may not wish to be associated with the views we have expressed: Jenny Backwell, Henrietta Dombey, Ken Fines, Jim Hennessy, David Harvey, Richard Kirkby, David Lipsey, Ian McGill, Michael Meacher, Steve Merrett, Stuart Morley, Jill Norman, John Payne, Peter Riddell, Les Robinson, Sigmund Sternberg, Ted Bowman, Maureen Clark, Theresa Lewis, George Nicholson, and many others in the North Southwark Community Development Group. Finally, we want to thank Janet Annis and Lorraine Esposito for giving up so much of their time to type successive drafts.

P J A
R J C

Introduction

This book is about property development. Our aim is to demystify and explain the workings of the property machine, particularly in relation to office development. We consider the part played by the financiers, the developers, and the agencies of central and local government. We also show why office development was so profitable up to the end of 1973 (and no doubt will be again), and what must be done if the system is to be changed. Although there was a temptation to write up the more racy details concerning individual developers, councillors, estate agents, and consultants (especially where an individual does not shrink from filling several roles at once), we have tried to avoid this. The defects of the system as a whole are more important than the individual cases of corruption and collusion evident within it. In any case, these aspects are fully covered by community papers all over the country.

Equally important, our aim is to relate redevelopment to the general debate about wealth inequality by asking *who gains and who loses* from this process. Studies have shown that wealth is very unequally distributed in Britain and no one has yet refuted the conclusion reached by Atkinson from a comparison of the wealth distribution in various developed countries that

It seems quite possible that, as far as the distribution of wealth is concerned, Britain has the doubtful distinction of leading the international inequality league.

The reasons for this state of affairs have been documented in many studies but one process which has so far escaped investigation is the way in which the property system benefits almost exclusively the wealthiest sections of our society. Many of the most important types of tangible wealth are closely related to the land and property system. A recent study of wealth by Fleming and

Little indicates in passing that over 60% of personal wealth has links with property – houses, land, insurance and pension rights, and shares being most significant. In later chapters, we shall explore some of these links for the country as a whole and for two case studies of redevelopment, in Brighton and Southwark.

In addition, we shall be concerned with the less easily measured but extremely important social costs of the development process. Since buildings normally last about seventy to a hundred years, something between 1% and 2% of the total stock of buildings is likely to be renewed each year under normal economic circumstances. This is a massive amount of rebuilding and much of it occurs in the Victorian inner suburbs of our major cities. Typically, the areas affected have a mix of old terraced houses or tenements, factories, warehouses, corner shops, and pubs, and are occupied by lower-paid residents and workers. If this land, by virtue of its proximity to the city centre, is re-zoned for 'higher' and 'more intensive' activities (terms which are synonymous with more profitable land uses), the social costs fall most directly on the local community.

We have directed our attention to urban redevelopment not only because we suspect that its costs and benefits are unfairly distributed but also because it exhibits a discrepancy between widely held myth and probable reality. Local authorities like Brighton and Southwark point to their success in attracting 'wealth' to the area in the form of office developments, leisure complexes, hotels, trade marts, theatres and conference centres. With the increased rate revenue, they declare, housing and social services can be provided for those in greatest need. Our case-study material exposes the defects of this argument. There is no guarantee that the increased revenue will be used to help the most needy. Commercial development uses scarce land that could have been used to house those on the steadily lengthening waiting lists. Leisure complexes and office blocks often bid up rents and living costs in the area by generating extra demands on the local housing system. People who lose their jobs because of 'asset stripping' have to pay extra commuting costs to reach jobs further afield. And, in any case, the extra costs to the rates of a housing crisis that lands more families in bed-and-breakfast and more children in care must be considerable. It may well be more than the extra rate revenue arising from redevelopment.

Several recurring themes run through all this. The poor get squeezed out to other areas or have to commit more of their earnings to necessities like rents and fares. The local housing scarcity which is maintained is good for the local property lobby since it means values and rents are kept up. And the profits from the process flow to capital, not labour. Several hundred people have become property millionaires since the last war; so far as we know, none have been building workers.

At the end of our general criticism of the present system (Chapter 6), we reassert what others have been saying for a hundred years. The task of determining the use to which a piece of land is to be put is not a technical one. It is a profoundly political one because it embodies a basic conflict between different interests. Typically, the interests of the land and capital owners are ranged against those of the would-be user. One is acting in accordance with an economic imperative and wants the highest possible financial return. The other needs housing or some other socially important facility at the lowest possible cost. Wants against needs; owners against users; the conflict can be stated in a number of ways. Both groups have aims which in the present political structure are perfectly justifiable. What is not justifiable is that people should seek to obscure or deny the conflict.

This book tries to remove the smokescreen from the issues and to present material that might encourage more public debate about the way the property machine works and the fundamental conflicts involved. Many of those engaged in redevelopment like to present it as a socially responsible activity and as 'progress' for the town or city in question. Sometimes it may be, but that depends on one's definition of progress. On the whole it seems unwise to leave that sort of judgement to those who are making a lot of money out of it. In any case, the notion of progress for the town, city, or the nation as a whole is a dubious one. It assumes either that the interests of all groups coincide or that, where they differ, all interests are adequately safeguarded by the democratic system of government. There is ample evidence in the book to show that both assumptions are wrong.

Chapter 1 Office Development – Rents, Values and Profits

Since all kinds of buildings – houses, offices, shops and factories – become obsolete or decay, urban redevelopment is a continuous process in all cities. It does not follow that the 'mix' of new buildings should exactly match the old pattern in any given part of the city or in the city as a whole. Change occurs in employment patterns and in shopping and recreational activities, while educational and health service expansion may entail an increase in the proportion of total built space that must be given over to schools, colleges, clinics and hospitals. Therefore to argue, for example, that all office building should stop and that all constructional resources should go to housebuilding, might lead to a situation where more people had a house but some had nowhere to work.

The main aim, from a general social welfare point of view, is to achieve an acceptable balance between the various types of development so that the total built space created fits, as well as possible, people's needs for living, working, being educated and enjoying themselves. In a centrally directed economy, with the economic imperative removed, it should be possible to calculate these various space requirements with reasonable precision and to ensure that, when part of a city is redeveloped, the rebuilt space complements the existing space in order to meet society's needs as closely as possible. But the present redevelopment system in Britain does not appear to achieve this, as a brief consideration of recent trends in the provision of housing and offices, to take two important types of development, will show.

Housing development

There is no need to belabour the point that Britain is experiencing a chronic housing crisis. Virtually every major city, and almost all London boroughs, have housing waiting lists that run into hundreds and thousands of families. The situation has been documented, analysed, and publicized so thoroughly that nobody can be in any doubt about what needs to be done; more housing needs to be built. The housebuilding record of recent years shows that, far from improving, the situation is getting worse.

Housing units completed, Great Britain (public and private) 1965–74

1965	382,000
1966	386,000
1967	404,000
1968	414,000
1969	367,000
1970	350,000
1971	351,000
1972	319,000
1973	294,000
1974	269,000

Source: *Housing and Construction Statistics*

The result of this appalling record is that the number of homeless people is almost certainly increasing. There is no one definition of homelessness since so much depends on factors that are culturally and socially determined. For example, are a young couple who are forced to live with in-laws because they can find no home of their own actually 'homeless'? Not by the standards of officialdom since they have not presented themselves to a housing department for emergency accommodation. But Shelter, the national campaign for the homeless, does define them as being homeless. And by Shelter's definition, which includes, loosely, all those who are precluded by their housing situation from living a 'civilized family life', there are actually millions of homeless people. Even taking the narrow definition of the number of people in emergency accommodation, the incidence of homelessness doubled between 1966 and 1971.

Apart from the drastic shortage of housing, much of it is below statutory standards. The 1971 Housing Condition Survey of England and Wales found that 7·3% of all housing units were unfit for habitation. This represents one dwelling in every fourteen. Even more strikingly, in the 'other tenures' category, which roughly corresponds to the privately rented sector, the unfit percentage was 22·9%. The significance of this figure is that the inner suburban areas of major cities, the areas most frequently affected by massive redevelopments, often have a greater than average incidence of this sector and thus an especial need for decent housing replacement rather than new offices. Both Southwark and Brighton/Hove, the two case-study areas chosen, have housing problems of frightening proportions, with housing waiting lists of over 9,000 and 2,400 respectively. These problems will be examined more closely in Chapters 4 and 5.

Office development

In contrast to the rate of house building, office development has been going ahead strongly in the past five years. The total national stock of office space increased from about 281 million sq. ft in 1967 to 340 million sq. ft in 1972, an increase of about 21% in five years. An increase of 21% in the total housing stock over the period would have been more than enough to solve our housing problem several times over. Of course, the absolute magnitudes involved are rather different. But if even half of this new office development had been built as housing instead, hundreds of thousands of extra people could have been housed.

In 1967 41·9% of the value of new orders obtained by contractors was for housebuilding and 2·4% was for private offices. In 1973 the proportions had changed considerably; only 35·1% was for housing and 7·5% was for private offices. The significance of these swings can be judged from the fact that the proportion of spending on other forms of development, for example factories and shops, varied much less over the six-year period. In 1973 the amount invested in offices was nearly 23% of the total spent on housing. In the light of the gravity of the housing crisis it is reasonable to ask whether this is an allocation of investment which society as a whole finds acceptable.

Even within the housing sector, a gap has opened up between investment in private and local authority housing. Private building has continued to show a healthy growth in orders placed, whereas from 1970 on the growth rate in local authority orders has been much slower. There are a number of reasons for this including the reluctance, or even the inability, of contractors to offer local authority work tenders that fall within the centrally specified cost yardsticks, which, in fact, from 1970 were updated much too slowly. Whatever the reasons for the disparity, the effects have caused widespread misery and housing stress. Those at the top end of the market have, as usual, not been seriously affected. Those who already own property have benefited from an increase in asset values due to the house price inflation that took place between 1971 and 1973. Those on middle-range incomes who aspire to buy have found that rapidly increasing prices and interest rates have made it difficult or impossible for them to do so. Those on lower incomes who qualify for council accommodation have found the waiting lists lengthening alarmingly, and those who do not qualify have had to compete in the privately rented sector with its widespread overcrowding, bad conditions and insecure tenures. The system that bears responsibility for these circumstances has much to answer for. The inputs of land, labour, capital and building materials which have been applied to the rapid growth of office space could for the most part have been applied to the construction of houses. The next section will seek to explain why they were not.

The Demand/Supply Situation for Office Space

The amount of profit to be derived from developing offices depends largely upon the present, and expected future, level of office rents. In the absence of rent control, which will be discussed later, rent levels tend to be largely dependent on the supply of office space in relation to the demand for it. The main factors conditioning the state of demand and supply therefore need to be examined.

Demand

As an economy develops, there tends to be a decrease in the proportion of the labour force employed in agriculture, mining and manufacturing and an increase in the proportion in what is known as the 'tertiary' sector. Roughly, this includes employment groups such as retailing, commercial, professional and personal services of all kinds, health, education, administration and so on. These groups between them tend to employ over half the total labour force in some 'advanced' countries. Service and administrative workers alone, all of whom work in offices, constitute over 35% of the British labour force in 1973 (see *Social Trends*). Many of them are engaged in activities which result from the modern tendency to transform operations which were previously quite simple, like paying money across the counter of a shop, into something much more complex involving credit cards, dockets in triplicate, monthly statements, debt recovery and credit rating. Those with an interest in raising the level of consumption, or in selling computers, are not unconnected with these tendencies. Whether or not these trends are ultimately beneficial to the economy is a question that raises a lot of complex issues. What *is* certain is that they lead to a steady growth in the demand for office space.

Not only are more and more people working in offices but each one of them is tending to use more space. It has been estimated that, because of the introduction of more and more business machines, the amount of space needed per office worker increases by something like 3% per year. Thus the demand for office space is increasing even faster than the number of office workers. For example, the Brighton Urban Structure Plan team calculated future space needs on the basis of 150 sq. ft per worker now, rising to 200 sq. ft per worker in the 1980s.

Another demand pressure, especially in the City and West End areas of London, stems from the recent growth of big multi-national companies and overseas banks. These institutions demand large amounts of prestige space wherever they operate and particularly in capital cities. They appear to be relatively unworried about the rent they pay, no doubt because rent is a fairly small item in their total budget. They are therefore instrumental in establishing new 'highs' in rent levels. Because of the collective operation of the office market, these 'highs' become norms a few years later.

In all, demand for office space has been at a very high level in recent years. Walton remarked that '. . . the current experience of estate agents dealing in West End offices seems to be that demand is very high . . .' while a report by R. Lionel and Partners, dated 1973, observed:

London is now suffering from its greatest ever dearth of office space and this situation is unlikely to improve in the immediate future . . . Inquiries for Central London offices have shown an increase of 45% over 1972.

The same report notes that there has also been a massive increase in inquiries from companies wishing to move out from the central area so that the ripple effects of the demand pressure for central space are likely to be felt in areas peripheral to the centre, in suburban areas and beyond. Prospects for developers in such areas are seen by the report to be excellent. In particular, 'In Southwark, a good many schemes are in progress . . .'

While demand for office space generally is strong, it is not equally strong for all types of offices. There seems to be a general acceptance that air-conditioned, prestige space in prime central locations in important financial centres will always attract clients and provide a sure hedge against inflation for the owners or lessors. But with increasing distance from the centre of the city, or from other offices and shopping centres, rent levels and asset values fall off sharply. Developers interested in producing new office space tend therefore to look for sites which are close to existing office complexes, so that 'face-to-face contact' may be possible between decision-makers in the various offices. They also want to be close to shops and pleasant open space, so that employees will be able to do their shopping, especially important for working wives, and have somewhere to walk during their lunch hour. These considerations are by no means trivial in determining the value of the final product, as a quick survey of advertisements for office space to let will show. The level of demand also depends upon the size of the unit of accommodation available. The recent rapid rise in rent levels has caused some institutions to decentralize clerical and secretarial workers but to seek small suites of offices in prestige locations for their executive staff. This has led a brisk demand for office suites of up to, say, 3,000 sq. ft in prime locations.

The government, ever since the outbreak of the Second World War, has been active in encouraging the decentralization of office work from London. The fear of bombing provided the first incentive, but subsequently the underlying reason has been the realization that the over-preponderance of a fast-growing office sector in London and the south-east has not helped policies designed to bring more employment growth to the regions. The government's latest attempt to lead by example was the commissioning of a report on the question of dispersing government work from the capital. The Hardman Report appeared in 1973 and proposed that 31,000 of the 144,000 civil service jobs in London could be relocated elsewhere. The Labour government subsequently implemented the report but with a greater stress on moving jobs to Development Areas. This would release something like 4½ million sq. ft of office space and might, conceivably, encourage private concerns to follow the example. Alternatively, to take a more worldly view, it might simply mean an addition to the stock of central offices for which advertising agencies, oil companies and finance houses can compete. The Location of Offices Bureau, the government agency set up largely to encourage the decentralization process, has been in existence for a number of years but its activities are confined to collecting information, offering advice on possible new locations and, at most, exerting gentle persuasion. It has been instrumental in helping to decentralize civil service and local government jobs but is obviously quite incapable of doing much to modify the demand pressures from the big international companies.

It was thought that our membership of the EEC would lead to an increased demand for office space but this has so far failed to materialize. A recent survey by R. Lionel and Partners of the 750 leading companies in Belgium, Holland, France and Germany resulted, surprisingly, in '. . . the overwhelming majority stating that they had no interest, either now or in the immediate future, in establishing an office in London'. The comparative review of office rent levels in Europe which follows later in this chapter may help to explain this.

Perhaps the main factor affecting the rate of office development
is the general one of the state of the economy and of the development sector in particular. In a period of high interest rates,
financial stringency, economic and political uncertainty and
general lack of confidence, investment funds may flow elsewhere
and development activity may slow down almost to a standstill.
All four factors are in operation with a vengeance at the time of
writing in late 1974. Many developments are being postponed or
cancelled and few completed blocks are changing hands. The
reasons for this, and some of its implications, will be examined
in detail later.

Various other factors conspire to restrict the supply of new
office space. Perhaps the most important of these are the controls
on development exerted by central government in the form of
Office Development Permits (ODPs) and by local government in
the form of planning consents. Both these will be examined more
closely in a later chapter. Briefly, ODPs apply to developments
of over 10,000 sq. ft in the south-east region and have to accompany planning applications for office development. They were
introduced in 1965 following the complete moratorium placed
on office development in London by George Brown in November 1964. The 'Brown Ban', as it was called, had quite unin-
tended effects. By restricting supply at a time when an office glut
looked likely, it sent rents upwards, saved a few over-extended
property companies, and made millionaires of those who happened to have planning consents in hand. It was, in fact, the
classic example, not unprecedented among government dealings
with the closelipped and complex world of property development, of using a hammer to regulate a watch.

Planning consents are granted by local planning authorities in
response to development applications. Authorities vary enormously, and sometimes unpredictably, in their readiness to grant
them. Similarly central government, in the shape of the Department of the Environment varies in its readiness to intervene by
calling in a development application and/or holding a public
inquiry as a result of an appeal against the local authority's
decision. Developers, as a group, have little doubt that it is these

governmental controls that play a decisive part in constricting supply, thus creating an 'artificial' shortage and pushing up rents. The Lionel report already quoted blames 'Office Development Permits (and) stringent planners who often do anything but plan . . .' for the rapid rise in rent levels and thus in values. There can be no doubt that this is largely true, although perhaps not many developers would agree with the corollary that if it is public action that is creating much of the value then maybe a good proportion of the value created should be at once returned to the public in the form of 'planning gain'.

Physical space constraints also apply in many cities. There is bound to be a shortage of development sites near the core of any densely built-up city especially if, as in the case of both London and Brighton, much of the central space is occupied by buildings of great historic or architectural significance. Central urban space is, by definition, scarce yet it is often the only kind of space that office developers are interested in.

It has sometimes been argued that developers have deliberately kept offices unlet so as to constrict supply and bid up rents. While a large unlet office block is offensive to many people and provides a rallying point for opponents of the property industry, as happened with the 1974 occupation of Centre Point in London, it seems that empty space constitutes only a tiny proportion of the total, perhaps 2% or 3% in most cities. This is likely to have, at most, a marginal effect on the supply situation. The activities of local pressure groups may, ironically, be of greater significance. By delaying office developments, or even achieving their cancellation, they may actually be instrumental in increasing the rental, and the value, of existing blocks in the area. If, however, pressure group activity turns the development into one that provides, for example, a range of manufacturing jobs more in accord with the pre-existing job structure in the area, then a great deal may have been achieved.

Rents, Values and Profits

Office rent levels, in the absence of government controls, are the result of the interplay of the demand and supply situation. Because of recent trends in many of the factors that have been discussed, and perhaps especially because of the degree of public control exerted over the rate of office production, rent levels in Britain are among the highest in the world. Some idea of comparative levels can be gauged from the following figures from the Counter Information Services report *The Recurrent Crisis of London*.

	Annual rent per sq. ft for first-class office space 1972
London (City)	£10.00
London (West End)	8.50
Paris	8.00
New York	4.00
Brussels	2.50

The figures for London are already out of date. The Lionel report, dated October 1973 quotes the following rents for new space: the City £20, Mayfair £13, Victoria £10, Holborn £9 and Kensington £5. By November 1973, a Japanese financial institution was reputed to have taken space in the City for £25 per sq. ft. Rent levels outside London do not approach these extremes. Prime space in Croydon may currently cost up to £8, in Bournemouth up to £4, in Brighton up to £3 and in Birmingham, Leeds and Bristol up to £2.50. All these figures are anything up to double what they were only a few years ago. It is extremely difficult to say what will happen to rent levels in the future since the threat or the reality of rent control tends to colour the market's expectations. But given the underlying demand pressures in relation to any likely rate of increase in supply, and the collective interest that most participants have in maintaining levels, it seems that they are unlikely to fall much, if at all. What seems more likely is that the present constrictions on supply will, when faced with a pent-up demand, lead to another move to new levels.

The step that equates the *annual rental* of a building to its *value* is a crucial one and is the key to the understanding of the wealth created by development. Given an annual rent or 'rack rent' of say, £1 million for a building, agreed for a seven-year period, and disregarding annual maintenance outgoings, what would an investor be willing to pay for the property? If he wanted an annual return of 10% on his money, he would be prepared to offer £10 million. In other words he would be ready to pay ten 'year purchase' (YP). But that is to assume that rents will remain at current levels for the life of the building, whereas if past trends can be relied upon they should double by the time of the next rent review, giving a return on capital invested of 20% (£2 million annual return on an outlay of £10 million). If this is the general expectation, there is likely to be competitive bidding for the building and the present value may be pushed up to £20 million, or twenty YP. This gives an initial yield of only 5% (£1 million annual return on an outlay of £20 million) but the likelihood is that this will double in only seven years and continue to increase thereafter as higher rents are fixed at subsequent reviews. If this can be relied upon, a purchaser will be prepared to put up with a low initial yield on the expectation of a much greater rate of return in the future.

What has happened in recent years, with the explosive growth in rent levels, is that investors have competed to bid up the prices at which office blocks change hands, thus bringing down initial yield levels. Properties that are not on the market are, of course, valued in accordance with prevailing YP norms, or, to put it another way, in line with current yields. If rents are rising, and yields are concurrently falling on the expectation of *future* rent rises, then the valuation of a building rises at a rapid rate. An example taken from the Lionel report already quoted should make the process clear (the figures relate to a building of 5,000 sq. ft and assume, for the sake of simplicity, that an annual rent review is possible):

Year	Rental (per sq. ft)	Annual rent revenue	Expected yield	Valuation
1971	£5	£25,000	7.0%	£360,000
1972	£6	£30,000	4.5%	£667,000
1973	£9	£45,000	5.0%	£900,000

Even though the yield had drifted up a little between 1972 and 1973 (in other words it was expected that a purchaser would pay only twenty rather than 22·2 times the annual revenue to acquire the building) the asset valuation still rose by 250% over the two-year period. These figures are by no means exceptional for a London example although 5,000 sq. ft is a very small office block. The space, and thus the valuation, should be multiplied by about twenty to get more typical figures. The gain in value over the period would then be not £540,000 but £10.8 million and this, in a slightly more complex form, is the revaluation that would take place on the assets side of the company's balance sheet between 1971 and 1973. Of course, if the company owning the building is a big one, and owns a number of other similar blocks, the annual revaluation might involve very large figures indeed. For example, the offices at Euston Centre owned by Stock Conversion and Investment Trust (Mr Joe Levy's company) rose in value from around £15 million in 1964 to nearly £74 million in 1972. Mr Levy did not actually have to do anything to bring about this rise in value. It all stemmed from the growth of rent levels in the area from £1.75 to £6.50 per sq. ft and the concurrent fall in yield from 6% to 4.5%. (See Counter Information Services report.)

The relationship between annual rental and asset valuation, in other words the yield level, is a complex one. It depends upon past trends in rent levels and perhaps even more on future expectations about rents, and especially about what the government's attitude to rent control might be. It also depends upon expectations about governmental tax policy. Up to the time of writing, in late 1974, no tax is paid on the unrealized gains that result from the annual revaluation of property owned. Tax is levied only when the building is sold and a capital gain made. An attempt was made in 1974 to tax part of the difference between cost and the notional capital value at the point when the building was first let. But this measure was generally unsuccessful and is soon to be dropped. It would not, in any case, have affected revaluation gains subsequent to the first letting. A tax on the subsequent increase in value would have a number of consequences, one of which would be a general dampening of the rate at which the balance-sheet value of buildings was written up.

This would cause yields to rise, assuming trends in rents remain unaffected, because the YP, or ratio of value to rent, would have fallen, reflecting the reduced attractiveness of ownership.

Property values also depend upon the general pattern of investment preferred by the lending institutions, whose behaviour will later be examined in detail. These institutions have a choice between three main forms of investment; stocks and shares (equities), government securities (gilt-edged), and property. If the first two grow in attractiveness compared to the third, perhaps because of fears of political or economic risk in the extremely volatile property sector, then the flow of funds into the development and purchase of office blocks may be reduced. Or even if the total flow of funds into property remains unchanged, shifts may occur between the proportion of investment going to its main components: offices, shops and industrial premises. If few investors are seeking to buy office blocks then naturally their value is reduced no matter what figures appear on the balance sheet. On the other hand, if the pace of office development slackens, the value of existing blocks will tend to rise and lead once again to lower yields.

Valuation is an extremely technical matter and it is not possible here to do more than sketch the main outlines of the process. For *freehold properties*, the main considerations in arriving at a value have already been sketched. These include current rent levels and expected trends in these levels, the location of the building and its standard of construction, general expectations about the future of the economy and expectations about future tax, planning and rent control legislation. For *leasehold properties* the problem of valuation has extra dimensions. If the lease is a long one, with a long period before the next rent review, the same factors predominate as with a freehold building. But if the lease has a short life, and/or frequent reviews of ground rent have been agreed, the problem is much more complex. The value of the *freehold* itself depends upon a number of factors including the 'hope' value of negotiating a much more profitable new lease, with much higher ground rent, in the near future. Thus an investor may possibly purchase the freehold for up to fifty or a hundred times the present annual ground rent (i.e. a yield of 2%

or 1%) on the expectation of a large increase in ground rent in the near future which would increase the yield to competitive levels. The value of the *lease* to an investor would depend on yet another set of factors, including the chance of a profitable short-term sub-lease arrangement at a current rent level which might show a large profit on the small amount being paid on a very out-dated ground rent. The YP figure is likely to be much lower because rent income will be received only for a limited number of years and an annual sinking fund will need to be provided out of rents to replace the capital value lost when the lease ends. Yet another complication arises if, on first selling the building, the original developer had secured an interest in the growth of its asset value and/or its future rental revenue. In either case this naturally reduces the attractiveness of the investment to a subsequent purchaser and affects the valuation.

It is impossible to over-stress the importance to the property market of the relationship between rents and values. If for any reason a number of buildings change hands at values which imply, say, a 25% worsening in the general ratio between values and rents, then the implication could be that all similar properties are worth 25% less than their balance-sheet valuations. For most property companies, property constitutes the major part of their assets so the implications for the assets side of the company's balance sheet are obvious. The company's liabilities, however, remain unchanged since they are mostly shareholders' funds and money loaned by banks or lending institutions on the security of the company's assets in order to carry out further developments. Thus if assets are over-valued, the company's position begins to look very suspect.

Another problem is that loan repayments at a time of extremely low yields and high interest rates are a constant heavy burden. If it suddenly becomes clear that the assets upon which the loans are secured are over-valued by, say, 15% to 25%, the lenders may press for repayment to protect their position. The company then has no option but to try and realize some of its assets. But its assets are principally large buildings which cannot be disposed of immediately at the best of times. At a time when the instincts of both buyers and sellers are to hold off, because everyone is fearful of the implications of a very low price, the company may simply be unable to meet its short-term commitments. This is known as a cash flow or liquidity crisis. The company may not actually be insolvent, because it may have a sound long-term relationship between assets and liabilities assuming the market recovers. But it is illiquid; it cannot pay its short-term bills and loan repayments.

Both these problems hit the property industry during late 1973 and 1974, especially in relation to office property. For example, John Ritblat's British Land Company increased its borrowings from £98 million to £175 million in the year to March 1974. At current interest rates it faces interest payments of £20 million or more per year. This has led to severe cash flow problems, a virtual shutdown of development activity, and a share price of 20p against a share value of 284p suggested by balance-sheet valuations (*Investors Chronicle*, 6 September 1974).

The production and sale of most commodities follows a relatively logical pattern. The article is produced at a certain cost and the price to the consumer reflects this cost plus an extra component for profit. This profit reflects the return to the manufacturer, wholesaler and retailer. Since most commodities are fairly substitutable, competition between producers for the favour of consumers is believed to act to some extent to keep prices and profit margins within acceptable limits. This logic tends to break down to some extent when the final product appears to have a value which is in some way unique or appears socially indispensable. Final price may then have little relationship to total production and distribution cost. Pharmaceuticals, for example, often come into this category.

The logic breaks down entirely in relation to office blocks. Their value, either in the sense of a balance-sheet valuation or in terms of the price at which they actually change hands, has little or no direct connection with the original cost of their creation and to this extent they resemble a Rembrandt portrait. The chain of reasoning that produces a current valuation or price has been outlined and no mention has been made of the cost of the main inputs: land, labour, capital and materials. It is impossible here to go into these costs in any detail. Labour, capital and materials can be costed with fair precision since wage rates, interest rates and material costs are known, although in periods of rapid inflation careful calculations have to be made about likely increases in costs over the life of the development.

Land is more difficult to cost. For example, the developer may be building on his own freehold, acquired in bits and pieces over a long period at outdated cost levels. One important consideration then is the 'opportunity cost' of using the site for one sort of development as opposed to a possibly more profitable alternative. But since recently there have been no more profitable uses than office development, there has been little opportunity costs involved in office development. Another possibility is that the developer is bidding for the lease on a piece of development land owned by a local authority. In this case the amount of ground rent offered, often in a bid in competition with other developers, is arrived at by making the calculation shown in a rather simplified form below:

Expected rent from tenants on completion of the building (rack rent)		£150,000 p.a.
Less annual outgoings (on an expected total building cost of £1,000,000)		
– annual loan repayments on long-term loan of £1,000,000 at 8%	£80,000	
– annual return for profit and risk at 2% on £1,000,000	£20,000	£100,000 p.a.
Therefore ground rent offer to local authority		£50,000 p.a.

Alternatively, if the local authority is looking for ready money to finance other work, it may specify to competing developers that it wants a premium in cash of, say, £200,000 immediately, but is willing to accept a lower ground rent. The calculation may then look like this:

Expected rent from tenants on
completion of the building
(rack rent)   £150,000 p.a.

Less annual outgoings

– expected total building cost	£1,000,000	
– premium to local authority	£ 200,000	
	£1,200,000	
– annual loan repayment on long-term loan of £1,200,000 at 8%	£ 96,000	
– annual return for profit and risk at 2% on £1,200,000	£ 24,000	£120,000 p.a.

*Therefore ground rent offered
to local authority* (plus the
premium of £200,000 in cash)   £30,000 p.a.

In either case it can be seen that the ground rent offer, and
thus the land cost to the developer, is a *residual* figure. It is
very important to grasp that land value is an almost meaningless idea except in terms of the use to which the site can be put.
Land has no value in a use vacuum since profitability is so
heavily contingent on use. In the calculations shown, the main
variables are expected rent levels and construction costs, the
rate of interest that needs to be paid for the finance, and finally
the rate of profit the developer is seeking. This profit is, of
course, only a tiny part of what the developer stands to gain.
The value of the asset he is creating is, in all normal conditions,
likely to appreciate vastly and rapidly.

The same sort of logic is likely to dictate the bid a developer
might make to purchase a site, or the components of a possible
site, in order to develop it. But in this case there are many more
uncertainties. The planning consent and, if applicable, the
Office Development Permit (ODP), may not yet exist so that
the offer may include an element of 'hope value'. In other
words, it may be made in the expectation that a certain use will
be allowed in the future. This obviously opens up a variety of

situations in which a bidder is tempted to go to the legal limit, and quite possibly beyond, in his attempts to influence planning decisions made about the permitted use or uses on the site.

The example of the Tolmers Square development in Euston, as reported by Counter Information Services, may help to illustrate the order of difference between the costs and the value of office development. The development company concerned is Stock Conversion who acquired the nine-and-a-half acre site over a ten-year period from 1962. Camden Council, the authority involved, have the drastic housing problems common to most Inner London boroughs. One solution would have been to acquire the Tolmers Square site for housing, but in view of the very high local land costs, partly brought about, of course, by the known interest of big commercial redevelopers in the area, it seemed unlikely that central government approval would be forthcoming for a Compulsory Purchase Order (CPO) on the site. As a result various negotiations took place to allow the developers to continue with their scheme in return for a 'planning gain' to the Council in the shape of the sale of some of the site back to the Council for housing development. For present purposes, the significance of this situation lies in the calculations made in 1973 by the Council of the cost of the development to Stock Conversion in relation to its value on completion (at almost every point in the Council's calculations the assumptions err in the direction of understating this cost/value difference).

Total cost of land		£ 7,000,000
Less: land sold to Council		£ 1,700,000
		£ 5,300,000
Cost of interest on loans (for land)		£ 1,594,000
Demolition and construction costs:		
offices	£6,100,000	
shops etc.	£1,640,000	£ 7,740,000
	Cost of bridging loan	£ 774,000
Total costs		£15,408,000

The Council calculated the annual revenue as follows (in 1973):

Offices (190,000 sq. ft at £6 per sq. ft)	£1,140,000
Shops etc. (108,000 sq. ft at £1.75 per sq. ft)	£ 189,000
Car spaces (200 at £200 per car)	£ 40,000
	£1,369,000

Assuming yield levels of, say, 5%, which was about right at the time, the value of the completed building would be twenty times the annual revenue (twenty YP). This gives an asset value of about £27.5 million. Assuming even a modest rise in office rents in the area to £8, the value becomes about £35 million. In the former case the difference between cost and value is £12 million; in the latter it is £20 million. Both figures are so astonishing as to be almost meaningless.

The nature of the wealth created

The value of the development industry as a whole has multiplied many times in recent years. In 1958, the combined stock market valuation of all property companies was £103 million, in 1968 it was £833 million, and in 1972 it was £2,644 million. To take one case, it was widely quoted in 1973 that Mr Hyams of Oldham Estates was worth £300 million as opposed to £27 million in 1967. What does this increase in value actually denote? It certainly does not reflect Mr Hyams's worth to society. This wealth may be either the balance-sheet valuation of his company's assets or it may be, in the case of companies quoted on the stock market, the value quoted for the company's share. In neither case can it readily be converted into a pile of banknotes since, whether visualized as buildings or as shares in a company, realization into other more usable forms of wealth depends upon finding willing cash buyers.

To this extent the wealth is paper wealth. The statement that a company is worth £300 million (rather than £100 million more or less) depends on a number of shared assumptions among those who operate in the system. These include assumptions about the future state of the economy and the actions of government, about the competence and business reputations of those directing the enterprise, and about future trends in the demand/supply situation for property of various kinds. All these assumptions are bound up with the shadowy ideas of confidence and risk. There appears to have been little systematic study of the collective behaviour and interaction of the relatively small handful of people who make the big investment decisions for the financial institutions. But since they are no doubt quite well known to each other, if not personally, then by reputation, it seems reasonable to assume that once a few of them begin to question some of the key assumptions upon which a company's wealth depends, then very quickly further investment in that company will appear risky. Most investment decisions at any level tend to trade off returns against risk. A high risk will only be accepted if returns appear to be high. Once a company is seen to be a high investment risk, it will have to offer the inducement of yet higher returns in order to attract the necessary further finance. It may then be driven to decisions and developments which are ill judged and cause a sudden, and possibly complete, evaporation of the wealth detailed on its balance sheet.

We might also ask whether or not this wealth is productive to society. Does it produce further material goods or intangible satisfactions, as for example a production line or a Beethoven quartet do? It appears not. It seems that the sole use of the extra £100 million involved in valuing a company at £400 million rather than £300 million is that extra funds may be borrowed from financial institutions on the strength of it. Whether or not this extra money is put to productive use depends upon what is done with it. If it is all used to build new factories, schools or hospitals one can see that it has been a productive investment, provided of course the new buildings are quickly put to use. If it is used to tear down an old, but perfectly usable, office block and replace it with another, or to produce a large building that stands empty for years, society may doubt the wisdom of the system.

Chapter 2 # Finance Capital and the Development Industry

As we saw in the previous chapter, redevelopment activity depends upon money borrowed from the large financial institutions. This chapter examines the structure of the development industry and the complex and changing relationship between developers and their sources of finance. It also considers the investment pattern of the various kinds of institutions which, collectively, constitute the world of finance capital.

The Development Industry

The existence of a development industry is a relatively recent phenomenon. Before the Second World War there were very few large property companies. Instead, redevelopment was undertaken by individual entrepreneurs, or by firms developing buildings for their own occupation. There were few speculative office blocks and the tendency was for firms to own freeholds to their premises rather than rent. Certainly, there was no public awareness of 'developers' as such. Few property companies were quoted on the Stock Exchange, there was virtually no property press dealing with commercial development, and there was no coherent organization lobbying for the developers.

After the war all this changed. The property boom began with the reconstruction of bombed-out town centres and as it secured an increasingly powerful place in the economy, development companies proliferated along with estate agents, surveyors, and property investment companies. During the 1950s and early 1960s property tycoons such as Charles Clore and Jack Cotton of City Centre Properties flourished. Similar one-man empires still exist, notably Harry Hyams of Oldham Estates and Joe Levy of Stock Conversion and Investment Trust, but the trend is towards the creation of large development combines with shares quoted on the Stock Exchange.

With the increase in size of property companies and the obvious financial significance of property development, financial institutions have established formal links with property companies and property investment companies. Thus, in sharp contrast to the small developer of pre-war days, the development industry is increasingly dominated by giants such as Land Securities Investment Trust, Metropolitan Estate and Property Corporation, and the developer institutions such as the Prudential, Norwich Union, and Eagle Star.

These giants are the product of a steady process of takeovers and mergers since the 1950s. Companies have taken over weaker but asset-rich rivals, while the financial institutions have moved in on the development companies to consolidate their own asset bases and to take a share in the profits from the development boom. Thus, Land Securities became the largest UK property company when it took over the huge City Centre Properties of Cotton and Clore in 1966. More recently, one of the largest UK property groups, Town and City Properties, bought Central and District Properties from a finance group called Keyser Ullman and was then itself taken over by Sterling Guarantee Trust with the Prudential Assurance Company, the financial backer of both Town and City and Sterling, standing in the wings ready to move in if Sterling gets into trouble. Other examples of conglomeration are the takeovers of Sterling Estates by Royal Insurance, of Cavendish Land by Legal and General Insurance, and of Edgers Investments by the Prudential.

Though it is almost impossible to draw the line between property companies, construction companies, banks, insurance companies and investment trusts, some idea of the size of development companies in the UK can be gained from a listing of twelve top quoted property companies measured by their share valuation on the Stock Exchange.

The top twelve UK property companies (Sept. 1974)

£m Capitalization	Company
166.3	Land Securities Investment Trust
108.3	Metropolitan Estate and Property
87.8	St Martins Property
40.9	Hammerson Group
38.8	Great Portland
35.1	Slough Estates
34.7	Town and City Properties
31.2	Artagen Properties
24.5	Amalgamated Investment and Property
23.7	Haslemere Estates
22.4	Stock Conversion and Investment Trust
21.1	Berkeley Hambro

Even though this valuation was taken at a time of recession in property, the value of the top three property companies exceeded the value of many of the largest industrial firms in the country including Bowaters and British Leyland.

In addition to the large property concerns there are hundreds of smaller property companies. Many of these are one-man firms or offshoots of estate and insurance agents. Others are subsidiaries of the larger companies. For example, the St Martins Property Company, itself taken over by the Kuwait Government in 1974, has twenty-seven wholly owned subsidiaries in the UK and fourteen overseas, mainly in Australia. Amalgamated Investment and Property has twenty-three wholly owned subsidiaries in the UK and three overseas. While most of these subsidiaries are actual operating property companies, there are also countless paper property companies that have been formed for tax purposes. It is quite common for a property company to register a separate company simply for the purposes of undertaking one development or property transaction.

Overall a pattern has evolved of conglomeration at the top with a proliferation of subsidiaries at the bottom; in other words, a pattern that parallels other industries in the UK, though arriving a little later in the case of property development because finance capital did not fully begin to grasp the profit-making potential of redevelopment until after the war. But now the trend has gone so far that Mr Sydney Mason, Chairman of the Hammerson Group, has predicted, with some exaggeration perhaps, that there will be no property companies left by 1980. Instead, large firms, institutions, and investment trusts will retain their own property experts. This absorption of the old-style development industry by the finance sector has given the property industry considerably more bargaining power and consequently makes any form of state intervention more forbidding.

Less visible than the property companies but nonetheless important, is the involvement of industrial and commercial firms in the sale and redevelopment of their own properties. Most large firms, from Brooke Bond to Burtons Tailoring have their own property subsidiaries. Naturally, those firms with prime high-street properties such as Woolworths, Marks and Spencer, the clearing banks, and department stores are particularly well placed for redevelopment activities. Nor has the potential of prime properties escaped public industries such as the Post Office or British Rail. The Post Office recently appointed a well-known property expert and financier, Sir Max Rayne, of London Merchant Securities, to review its property assets said to be worth over £500 million at cost alone.

During the property boom, many firms sold off some of their property assets or were bought out by 'asset-strippers'. A remarkable article on how to speculate on old industrial properties appeared in the *Estates Gazette* in 1971. It was entitled 'Hidden Gold'. Asset-strippers such as Jim Slater and John Bentley made their reputations and personal fortunes by buying industrial firms and selling off or redeveloping some of the properties. It was for this reason that Slater Walker bought the Law Stationery Society with its prime properties in the City of London. But equally, industrial firms undertook their own asset-stripping. The International Publishing Company, for example, bought a series of printing firms in Central London and proceeded to close them down successively and redevelop the sites for offices wherever possible.

Finance Capital

The development industry is a complex of interlocking financial institutions, construction firms, and landowners but at its heart lies a more imposing network of organizations. This network is called finance capital. Glyn and Sutcliffe in their book *British Capitalism, Workers, and the Profits Squeeze*, describe finance capital as those companies that make profits out of owning and trading stocks and shares, government bonds, and currencies, and by providing services such as insurance, pensions, hire purchase, and mortgages. This type of activity contrasts with industrial capital whose main activity is the manufacture and processing of goods and commodities.

Property development is closely related to finance capital. Part of this is due to the fact that property companies and individual buildings are worth so much more in financial terms than industrial assets. For example, early in 1974, the 280,000 sq. ft Commercial Union building in the City of London was worth over £100 million, which at the time, was twice as much as the capitalized value of British Leyland and was worth more than other industrial firms such as Pilkington Glass and Plessey.

The links with finance capital come into sharper focus when we examine what developers actually do. Their main task is to find the money for developments and to act as an intermediary between landowners, estate agents, planners and the financial institutions. Their job is to enable developments to take place through a series of negotiations and paper transactions. Since the resulting product, the development itself, is so valuable compared to the amount of work the developer has to do, the developers and the other interests involved make a great deal of money from doing very little. And because the developer is working at the same time on behalf of the banks and landowners, he acts as an agent for finance capital.

Moreover, the ties to finance capital continue once the development project is completed. Commercial buildings are extremely valuable financial assets and like any others are traded for investment and profit. Such is the value of buildings that they are sometimes sold in pieces to different investors. Thus, going back to the Commercial Union building, part of this was sold to a consortium in April 1974 for £31 million and another 44% to the Abu Dhabi Investment Board for £36 million in July 1974. To the finance world the principal interest in office buildings such as the Commercial Union is its value as a financial asset. Its value as a social or environmental asset is almost irrelevant unless that happens to influence the financial value.

Not all properties are good investments, however, and finance capital needs the assistance of skilled property investors to ensure that the correct judgements are made. Investors recognize three sub-markets in commercial property : industrial, shops and offices. These markets are distinguished principally by their yields or rates of return on investment. Thus, the average yield for industrial property between 1971 and 1974 was 9%, with shops at 6½% and prime offices at 5½%. As pointed out in Chapter 1, these differences in yield reflect the relative demand for investment property; investors are prepared to accept very low yields for office property because of its long-term rental growth prospects but want high returns from industrial property because of its more modest rental growth prospects and faster rate of obsolescence. These relative differences change with fluctuations in the demand for property. Although it is difficult to imagine that office developments have not always been supremely valuable, in the 1950s prime shops let to national multiples such as Marks and Spencer and British Home Stores produced better returns than offices. Less dramatic swings in yields take place continually and there are also important variations from one part of the country to another.

Another way in which the sub-markets in property are distinguished is by the relative rates of rental growth. During the property boom particularly between 1966–74 rents for all forms of property raced upwards reaching a peak in 1974. As with yields, rents vary considerably from one location to another. And although most of the publicity was captured by the spectacular rents asked for new office blocks in the City of London, rents for both shops and industrial premises experienced an unprecedented boom. Industrial rents in the south-east rose by 203% between 1966–74 while office rents in the south-east outside London rose by only 160%. In Greater London, office rents rose at the same rate as industrial buildings, except in the City where office rents rose by over 400% between 1966–74. (See Chapter 1.)

However, it is not the level of rents but rather the rate of rental growth, which is the most crucial part of the arithmetic of property development. This is why the property world likes to see at least a steady increase in office rentals if not an unrestricted boom. Even at the height of the boom in 1973 investors were hoping for still higher rents and prices for office blocks. The prominent estate agent Edward Erdmann makes the point in a report published in the *Estates Gazette* of 13 January 1974 that investors were paying prices for freehold properties in London that were twice those paid in 1971 and adds that 'we hope that there will be increased demand leading to high prices for offices in Central London'..

If yields, rents, and locations are considered together a clear ranking of investment property emerges, with Central London offices at the top of the list and industrial premises in secondary positions at the bottom. This is the basis for assembling a property portfolio. Typically, about half of the portfolio will be offices, shops about 17% and industrials about 27%. Measured by value, however, offices may make up over 70% of the portfolio. The geographical distribution by value usually shows a very high concentration in the south-east and especially in London. For example, the Abbey Life Property Bond Fund held the following portfolio in 1973 by value:

Central London	34.7%
Rest of south-east	31.3%
Midlands/East Anglia	12.1%
South-west and Wales	6.4%
North and Scotland	6.3%
Overseas	9.2%
	100.0%

With this sort of ranking, it is not surprising that one of the characteristics of the property market is that in spite of government policy towards the regions money pours into areas where the growth potential is greatest, while other areas, perhaps badly in need of redevelopment, are left untouched and derelict.

There are some other, though less important factors, that the property investor will consider. When choosing between individual buildings, or redevelopments the investor will be interested in both the tenure and tenancy of the property. Freehold properties are always more valuable than leasehold properties unless the lease happens to be very long, say over seventy-five years. The reason for the superiority of freeholds is that the freeholder controls the rents, disposal and redevelopment of the property. Investors are also attracted by what are known as reversionary properties or buildings that have an outstanding lease which is due to end within a few years, at which point rents can be pushed up, increasing greatly the value of the property.

High-quality tenants are of some significance to the investor because of the security and prestige that they bring. The Government is considered the best tenant of all though international corporations are regarded highly. Since these tenants are likely to be looking for properties in London and the south-east, this is yet another reason for the heavy concentration of property investment in the areas where land values and rents are already highest.

We may have given the impression that money flows into property simply because of its growth potential. But finance capital must make one other series of calculations before any money is committed to property and before the bank lends to a property company. These calculations concern the relative attractiveness of property compared with other financial assets. Property must compete with currency transactions, government stocks, ordinary shares, and the rates of return from depositing money with banks or building societies. It has frequently been said that property is a good hedge against inflation. Gilt-edged and government stocks selling at fixed rates of interest lose their value with rising inflation, while shares have been shown to lag behind the inflation rate taken over a fifteen-year period. Property values have on the other hand risen faster than the rate of inflation. The explanation sometimes offered for this is that land is a commodity which has a fixed supply, while the demand for land and property is always expanding. The result barring a complete collapse of the economy is a steady increase in land prices, rents, and property assets. This is something of a circular argument because it is finance capital which is partly responsible for stimulating demand for property in the first place, by its own needs for office space, by lending money to developers and by pouring money into property as a hedge against inflation. Nevertheless, it is a fact that over the last ten years, considerable long-term investment has gone into property because it is thought that there is 'nothing safer than bricks and mortar'.

The Banking System and the Property Market

We must now turn to the ways in which the institutions of finance capital lend money to developers. By far the most important source of finance for development is the banking system ranging from prestigious merchant banks to the clearing banks and fringe banks. All these banks lend money to property development directly or through subsidiaries. With high interest rates and a share in the equity from the development, the banking system made a lot of money out of property during the boom.

Some developers, for their own part, found ingenious ways to borrow large amounts of money from the banks. One of the most notorious, but by no means unique, property speculator companies was the Freshwater Group owned by William Stern. The Freshwater Group conducted its activities through an intricate network of 500 private companies and one of its most successful techniques was a variation on the process known as remortgaging.

For example, the company bought a shop and residential block in North London at a cost of £72,000. Freshwater obtained a £55,000 mortgage and found the extra £17,000 itself. The rents of the shops and flats were immediately pushed up so that yearly rental income rose from £5,480 to £9,026, which in turn meant that the capital value of the block rose sharply. Three years after purchase, the property was revalued at £115,000 and the company took a new mortgage on it, this time of £76,000. This was enough to repay the original mortgage and leave a surplus of £21,000. Thus, after three years, the company had paid back its first mortgage, had got back all its own investment plus a bonus of £4,000, and on top of all that had taken £27,000 in rent. It also held the property as an enormously valuable asset.

While this sort of ingenuity depended partly on rising property

45

values and on the power to increase rents, the banking system must also take responsibility. This is how the *Investors Chronicle* characterized the behaviour of the banks between 1971–3.

When historians review the events of 1971 to 1973 from a decent distance they will find it difficult to avoid the conclusion that the British banking ystem and its related institutions took leave of their collected senses. The money supply was increasing at an annual rate of 25% compound and much of the increase was being shovelled indiscriminately, greedily, and unproductively into investments such as property which could not possibly earn their keep with interest rates at 17–18%.
Investors Chronicle 23–9 August 1974

The figures for lending to property companies and construction companies tell the tale very clearly. Between 1968 and 1973 monthly average lending rose fourfold, as the table below shows.

Amounts outstanding to property companies and construction

£million – monthly averages for Feb., May, Aug., Nov.

	Property Companies	Construction
1968	347	371
1969	320	378
1970	336	443
1971	430	509
1972	888	816
1973	1,669	1,282

Source: *Financial Statistics*, February 1974

Fuelled by the sharp increase in the money supply under the Conservative government, the fringe banks rapidly increased in numbers and financial influence. They attracted money from the public by gimmicky schemes and high rates of interest on deposit accounts and then lent the money liberally. While the loans could only be retrieved over a fixed and usually long period, depositors could withdraw their money at any time. The banks were thus borrowing short and lending long.

One of the many classic examples of money lent in this way is the short saga of London and County Securities. This bank came on to the scene in 1969 and expanded very rapidly, so that by early 1973, not only were many of the company investments represented by property, but the company had loaned over £65 million mainly to property companies. When depositors withdrew their money and the property market slumped later in the year it was inevitable that London and County collapsed.

Many other finance groups lending money to property suffered the same fate. The names of these small firms have probably been forgotten already – Cedar Holdings, Moorgate Mercantile, Triumph Investment, for example. Their collapse may have hurt a very small number of people, but their significance is that they were the tip of the lending iceberg for property in which every finance group in the country from insurance to merchant banks was involved. The more respectable banks and institutions tried to give the impression that it was the fringe banks that had been irresponsible. But the clearing banks have always lent money to property companies and continued to do so during the monetary boom of 1971–3. The only difference was that the clearing banks had a much more secure asset base. The kind of property development that was financed was not significantly different. William Stern's companies did not need to go to a fringe bank to get support for their enterprises.

Nor were merchant banks any less responsible. For example, although the banking group of Keyser Ullman, chaired by Conservative MP Edward du Cann, appointed two property specialists to its board in 1972, and by mid 1973, one third of the group's total advances of £254 million were in property; yet one year later, the group was forced to set aside £17 million for bad debts to property. As we shall see later on, the giant insurance groups with strong financial links with the banking system, were also affected by this sort of lending and investment policy.

The government made some attempts to control the flood of money into property but their warnings came too late and appeared to have little effect. The first directive from the Bank of England came in August 1973. It asked the banks to slow down their lending to property companies. But during 1973 monthly lending from the banks actually rose beyond 1972 levels, so the Bank of England was compelled to issue a further directive in

September 1973. Shortly after that bank loans to property fell but unfortunately the Bank of England cannot take much credit for this. The main reason was the dramatic rise in minimum lending rates from $7\frac{1}{2}\%$ in June 1973 to 13% in November 1973. With uncertainty creeping into the property market, these were interest rates that few developers could afford.

The weakness of the government's intervention into the property finance system deserves further attention because it reveals some of the contradictions in the government's role. The directives came much too late to save the secondary banking system and were not in any case blanket restrictions on loans to property. For example, construction companies were exempt despite the fact that some of the largest construction companies are also development companies, for example, Wates and Laing. Also exempt were loans for sale and leaseback schemes. These are arrangements frequently used by insurance companies and pension funds by which the fund buys a site from a developer and grants him a lease and the resources to develop the site. Thus, although the government, and a Conservative one at that, realized that it was wasteful and inflationary to pour more money into commercial property, it was not prepared to do anything more than send a polite letter to the clearing banks. To have asked the banks and other institutions to withdraw from their commitments to the property sector might have brought the banks themselves down.

Insurance Companies in the Property Market

Most of the discussion so far has been about the banking system, but it must not be forgotten that insurance companies and pension funds are deeply involved in property as an investment. They lend money to property companies and also undertake their own property developments.

Insurance companies are much more selective than banks in their lending and investment policy. They lend money to large development projects undertaken by reputable property companies. The usual arrangement is for finance to be provided at a fairly low rate of interest compared to the bank rate, in return for which the insurance company takes a percentage of the rents from the completed building or agrees to buy the completed development at some discount. Sometimes, insurance companies and pension funds will buy land and lease it to a developer providing long term finance to cover the cost of the development. The institution sets the ground rent at a percentage of the rents from the completed building or takes a percentage of the rack rent as well as the ground rent. At the end of it all, the insurance company owns a valuable freehold asset against which it can borrow money. Increasingly, insurance companies are undertaking their own developments. Some have acquired the expertise by buying out property companies, others have established their own property divisions. With huge amounts of funds available for investment, insurance companies have considerable power over the fortunes of the property market.

The total value of insurance company holdings reached £19,101 million in 1972 and is increasing at a rate of £1,500 million a year. Most of this expansion is due to the dramatic boom in life insurance. Between 1970 and 1973, there was an explosion

£m net investments of insurance companies (life funds)

	Total	Land and Property	%
1968	895	119	13
1969	816	186	23
1970	972	196	20
1971	1,230	198	16
1972	1,618	131	8
1973	1,663	299	18

Source *Financial Statistics*, Table 75, no. 142, 1974

of new forms of life business. Marketed by small companies and insurance offshoots of large finance groups such as Hambros and Abbey Life, these new life policies were linked directly to the performance of unit trusts and in contrast with normal insurance arrangements, the premium could be withdrawn at any time. Thus life assurance became another form of financial speculation and though it was another manifestation of the monetary boom, it was nevertheless new income that insurance companies had to invest, and as a result, the annual net investments of life assurance companies doubled between 1968 and 1973 with property taking a large share.

Exactly how insurance premiums of all kinds are invested is of great importance. The total investment of insurance companies in 1973 had the following overall distribution:

Gilt-Edged Stock	40%
Shares	26%
Mortgages	15%
Property	13%
Other	6%

Although this was the average distribution in 1973, investment patterns vary the whole time. Because of inflation, gilt-edged stocks are at present relatively unattractive compared to shares but if the government indexes stocks to the rate of inflation, investment may move back into gilts. The amount of money destined for property has varied too. In 1969, as much as 23% went to property but in 1972 property investment accounted for only 8%. Mortgages to property companies are steadily increasing. It is interesting to note that during the height of the property boom in 1972 the insurance companies held back from property because they judged that they would be paying inflated prices if they went in when the boom was at its peak.

However, the involvement of insurance companies in land and property extends beyond the direct investment of policy-holders' money in development projects. Insurance companies also invest in property shares, property unit trusts, and the finance groups that support the developers. For example, the Prudential Assurance Company, the largest general and life assurance company in the UK, has £150 million to invest every year and is widely involved in the property system. It has a 27% stake in United Dominions Trust, a large finance group which lost £21 million on property lending in 1974. It also owns 17% of merchant bankers Keyser Ullman, another big loser on property in 1974. The Prudential has also lent £40 million to Town and City Properties to help it to buy Central and District Properties which is a company owned by Keyser Ullman. Also, the Prudential has acquired the property group Edger Investments and owns half of

Compass Securities. In 1973, out of a total net investment of £152 million, £55 million went to property compared with £48 million to government securities and £49 million to equities.

The Prudential is not unusual for a large insurance group. The Norwich Union, for example, has a property portfolio valued at over £200 million including projects in Europe and is undertaking several projects on its own, including the Woking Town Centre scheme. In 1973, Norwich Union invested a total of £38 million in property, telling its shareholders that this investment would offset the fall in share prices on the Stock Exchange.

Insurance companies are, however, not only interested in property as an investment. The large insurance companies are required by the Department of Trade to maintain a minimum 'solvency margin' of shareholders' capital and free reserves as a percentage of premium income, but increasingly insurance companies are finding it difficult to prevent this ratio from slipping. In order to build up shareholders' funds some companies have attempted to make takeover bids for property groups in the hope that the value of the shares of these companies will rise. For example, in 1974 Commercial Union made a bid, which turned out to be unsuccessful, for the St Martins Property Company because at the time the Commercial Union solvency ratio was well below the Department of Trade guidelines and, without maintaining the correct ratio, the company was restricted from seeking more insurance business.

These controls do not apply to the smaller insurance companies and some have paid the price dearly. During the monetary boom there was a proliferation of fringe insurance companies offering glamorous life policies with only flimsy asset bases to back up the policies. Companies such as Vavasseur Assurance, Cannon Street Assurance, and Nation Life folded rapidly when the property market slumped suddenly in December 1973. Nation Life, for example, owned just one principal asset; a development site in Bournemouth which had not yet received planning permission and which was virtually unmarketable.

There are no fears that the collapse of these fringe companies will affect the steady demand for general insurance and life assurance. In fact, other divisions of finance capital are eager to move in. The clearing banks are setting up their own insurance outlets, while the merchant banks, already behind life companies such as Hambros and Hill Samuel Life, are expanding and diversifying their insurance interests. With this expansion of business, more and more financial institutions are likely to be looking for places to invest insurance money and in the present circumstances property is likely to retain a high proportion.

Pension Funds in the Property Market

The total assets of pension funds are not far behind the insurance companies and are also growing rapidly. In 1972, while the insurance companies held assets worth £19.10 million, pension funds held almost £11,000 million and between 1968 and 1972, assets held by private funds rose by over 80%.

As with the insurance companies, pension fund investment in property has risen steadily. In 1967, pension funds had 4.7% of their funds in land and property but this rose to 11.3% in 1973, and each year over that period more money was invested in the property market. Moreover, the increase was not restricted to the private pension funds since all types of pension fund, whether a nationalized industry or a local authority fund, stepped up their commitment to property .

The largest pension fund of all is the Post Office Superannuation Fund. This Fund, with £170 million to invest every year is in fact the largest investing institution in the UK (the Prudential has only £150 million to invest annually). The total investments of the Fund in 1973 stood at £413 million of which 57.6% was in stocks and shares (29% in shares of finance and property companies), 22.3% in cash, 1.9% in fixed interest securities, and 18.2% in real property. Property investment totalled £27 million and had the following distribution.

Commercial property	£14,156,000
Industrial property	£101,000
Agricultural property	£697,000
Developments in progress	£11,984,000

These investments covered a wide variety of properties, all regarded as having long-term income potential. For example, in 1973, the Fund acquired English and Continental Property Holdings which consisted of forty properties including Bush House in the Aldwych in London. An agreement was also signed with Argyle Securities to make available £20 million over five years for developments in the UK. In addition, the Fund acquired a 1,000-acre agricultural estate in Yorkshire and a large estate of undeveloped land between Bognor Regis and Little-hampton in Sussex. Both estates belonged to the Marquis of Normanby.

All of this activity is undertaken by a relatively small group of investment managers on behalf of 40,000 contributing members. Pension benefits are paid out to 110,000 Post Office pensioners. It is interesting to note that income from the massive investments of the Post Office Fund account for less than a quarter of the money paid out every year to pensioners. Moreover, yearly income from contributors to the Fund dwarfs the amount paid out by a ratio of three to one. Therefore, one must conclude that the main function of the investments is to earn profit on the money flowing into the fund and is not essential to meeting the everyday needs of Post Office pensioners. If the Post Office Fund thought that they could earn the same rate of interest from banks or government stock as from shares and property, it would put its money there. It is not involved in property because it has any concern for homes, buildings or the environment. This is a quite incidental responsibility.

Exactly the same goes for the Coal Board Pension Fund. This fund has 64,000 contributors and pays out to 36,000 pensioners. The fund has risen from £240 million in 1969 to £340 million in 1973, of which £80 million or 28% was invested in property. To this large commitment to real property must be added £11 million in property shares (in mid-1973) and some quite heavy commitments to fringe banks which have lent to property. One of these banks, Cedar Holdings, has since collapsed, and the Coal Board Fund along with Unilever and Phoenix Assurance was forced to put up £72 million to pay off Cedar Holdings' liabilities. The Fund also lost £2 million because it bought shares in

Vavasseur Assurance, another fringe financial institution that folded.

There is, however, nothing permanent about this pattern of investment. After the shake-up and losses and sales of unattractive shares the pension funds will move their money into other fields. Already, the Post Office Fund holds 20% of its stocks and shares on overseas stock exchanges. In September 1974, a property investment group was established called the American Property Trust. Backed up by the Post Office, British Rail, British Steel, Electricity Supply Industry, and the National Westminster Bank, the trust will invest pension fund money in suburban office buildings and suburban shopping centres in the south-east of the USA. There are numerous other examples of contributions invested in overseas property, oil, farmland, and rapidly growing financial assets around the world. Nevertheless, once a pension fund has acquired a freehold interest in income-producing commercial property it is unlikely to let it go unless it is desperate for cash.

Property Bonds

Another vehicle for investment in property is the property bond. A property bond is really a life assurance scheme similar to unit trust life assurance but with the premium and the dividends tied solely to property development. Some of the developments will be undertaken directly by the fund but most of them will be undertaken by a developer with finance supplied by the fund and a share of the income returning to the fund.

During the financial boom, property bonds multiplied rapidly. Advertisements appeared in the press urging people to invest in property as a hedge against inflation and as the unit price of property bonds doubled between 1968 and 1973 the number of funds rose to thirty. Many of these funds were created by insurance companies and merchant banks. For example, Hambros Bank set up the Hambro Property Bond Fund, and United Dominions Trust spawned the Merchant Investors Fund. Others were offshoots of property companies and large corporations. Thus, Nation Life was part of the William Stern property empire, and Abbey Life is a subsidiary of the American giant, International Telephone and Telegraph Corporation.

Most of the funds are quite small and getting smaller while the property market is going through a recession. In 1973 only ten funds had assets worth more than £10 million, and the top three funds dominated the market.

	Abbey Property Bond	Hambros Fund	Property Growth
Properties	195	54	17
Income	£9.5m	£1.4m	£0.6m
Value	£195m	£70m	£45m

The average fund holds about 20% of its investments in cash as a hedge against fluctuations in the property market but the remainder is invested in prime commercial property with a strong preference for offices in the south-east. Some of the smaller funds have very little flexibility since policy-holders' money is tied up in only one or two properties. For example, the Tyndall Property Fund has £12 million of its £20 million fund tied up in one office building in the City of London. The result is that if commercial property is revalued downwards the fund is very vulnerable and cannot write more business. But since the collapse of the property market in 1973 property bonds have become relatively unattractive forms of investment or life assurance and many of them have merged for the meantime back into the insurance companies from which they came. Nevertheless, at the peak of the boom, property bonds acted as an important source of financing for commercial development and contributed to the trend for prime property to move into the hands of the financial institutions.

Equity Investment in Property

One of the traditional activities of financial capital is investing in shares on the Stock Exchange. Before the war, there were only ten quoted property companies in the UK, but there are now over 170 quoted property companies representing millions of pounds worth of shares. The value of this to the property companies themselves is that they can borrow against the capitalized value of their companies as if it was a tangible asset. Thus, the higher the share price, the easier it is to persuade a banker to lend money.

There are three ways in which money flows into property shares. First by the direct purchase of shares in a property company, second by investment in property unit trusts that spread funds through a portfolio of property shares, and third, by purchase of ordinary unit trusts that hold property shares along with non-property shares in a broad portfolio. Most of this investment in property shares comes from the institutions we have been looking at earlier. It has been estimated that 40% of all shares by value are held by the large institutions while on a daily basis, over 75% of the turnover handled by London brokers is undertaken on behalf of the institutions.

Nevertheless, funds from these sources vary with the fortunes of the general share market, though they also reflect variations in the quality of property companies themselves. During the property boom, property shares reached all-time highs. In June 1968 the Financial Times Property Index stood at about 100 points; by June 1972 it reached 200 points and touched 350 for a brief moment in October 1973, at the announcement by the Conservative government that they did not intend to introduce long-term control of business rents. In 1974, the index fell rapidly to its pre-boom level.

Even in the volatile world of commercial property some property firms are more attractive and secure than others. The largest companies such as Land Securities and MEPC are large enough to survive the steepest falls in the stock market. Some firms are in the 'blue chip' category, meaning that they have a steady business whatever the market fluctuations. Haslemere Estates, specializing in the renovation (for offices) of historic buildings, is one example. Firms that have a large percentage of property abroad or have a large income coming in from office rents on newish buildings are also considered good buys by the investment pundits.

The Taxation Advantages of Finance Capital

We have pointed out the main reasons why finance capital is involved in the property market but have not yet discussed the special taxation position of life assurance companies, authorized unit trusts, and pension funds. The general taxation position for ordinary companies at present is that large companies must pay tax on profits (Corporation Tax) at a basic rate of 52% with smaller companies paying 42%. In addition, ordinary companies pay tax on the disposal of assets (Capital Gains Tax) at a rate of 30%. On the other hand, authorized unit trusts and investment trusts pay Capital Gains Tax at a special rate of 15% while pension funds pay no Corporation or Capital Gains Tax at all. Prior to April 1973, life assurance companies paid Corporation Tax at their own special rate of 37.5%. This advantage was repealed but the fact remains that pension funds and unit trusts are charged a much lower rate of tax on property dealings whether it is the disposal of land or the profits from rent.

The Labour government of 1974 attempted to modify this position by proposing that pension funds and property unit trusts should pay Corporation Tax at the ordinary rate but this sparked off such a storm of protest from the National Association of Pension Funds and the Committee of Property Unit Trusts that the government backed down.

However, the taxation of development gains will change again under the Labour government's Land Bill. When the bill comes into effect, all companies including life companies and pension funds will pay a new tax called Development Land Tax which will replace all previous forms of taxation of development gains. This tax will probably be levied at 80% of the difference between the sale price or the market value of completed development and a base price which will reflect the use value of the site or building before the hope of development came about. It remains to be seen whether in the course of the lobbying that will take place on behalf of the financial institutions, life companies will obtain any concessions or pension funds and other charities will be exempt. It is worth noting that neither the traditional taxation of development gains nor the Development Land Tax apply to the increase in the capital value of land and buildings that are not being disposed of but are being held as investments. So from the investment point of view, the value of property is not damaged by this taxation.

Conclusions

Property development is firmly established as part of finance capital and in many ways development companies and financial institutions are virtually indistinguishable. The main reason for this is that property development cannot take place without large loans. Very few property companies have sufficient capital or income to undertake developments on their own since the income (from rents) received by property companies is very small in relation to the cost of developments. Repayments on huge loans create a constant demand for cash so that the only ways in which profits can be made are by raising additional mortgages and by selling off buildings and land.

The property system does not look upon property as an asset in a social or environmental sense. Property is a financial asset and the location and character of development are determined by investment criteria. And since finance capital invests only when and where demand and rents are rising, redevelopment has concentrated in selected areas such as London and the south-east and in particular types of development such as offices and shopping centres. Investors do not place their money in projects that are needed, but only into those that offer attractive profits. Thus, vast areas of land can lie derelict while other areas, perhaps not far away, are swamped with redevelopment even where buildings have many years of useful life left in them. The ultimate example of such waste is the recent case of a new office building in New York City which is being demolished because no tenant could be found for it; the cleared site being more valuable than the brand new building.

Since the mid 1960s the financial institutions have invested increasing amounts of money in land and property and in financial companies which have themselves lent large amounts to developers. Thus a large part of the asset base of finance capital is currently represented by property investment with the result that the financial institutions have an enormous vested interest in ensuring that property values continue to rise. Any intervention by the government in the property market is closely followed by the financial institutions and any move which threatens their interests is quickly and vigorously blocked.

Chapter 3

The Property Market
and the State

> . . . Contemporary capitalism has no more devoted and
> more useful servants than the men who help administer
> the State's intervention in economic life.
>
> Ralph Miliband, *The State in a Capitalist Society*

The planning system with its extensive legislation, thousands of
capital and property development but made no mention of planning and other functions of the state in this process. We shall
now turn to these functions and how they work in practice. The
main question that we will ask is who benefits from the present
system of state intervention.

The Planning System

The planning system with its extensive legislation, thousands of
local authority planners, and the massive bureaucracy of the
Department of the Environment is by far the most subtle of the
various interventions in development made by the state. This is
because the planning system has a very benign image, representing fairness and impartiality. If anything, there is a feeling
expressed by many especially in the business world, that the
system might be even fairer if there was a little less bureaucratic
intervention. Those who drew up the first comprehensive planning legislation after the war wanted it to be not only fair but to
give the general public more benefits from development than had
been forthcoming under a less restricted development system.
Thirty years later, it is rather easier to see the financial benefits
of the planning system than the social ones. Whose ends, therefore, is the planning system serving?

The machinery of planning control can be briefly summarized.
Under early town planning legislation most local authorities were
required to draw up a land-use map for their area to act as a
guide for considering development proposals. But by the mid

1960s most of these plans were out of date and almost every planning authority was seeking approval of official amendments from the Department of the Environment. As the amendments piled up and local authorities found themselves with no realistic land-use plans to go by, a new Planning Act was introduced in 1968 which authorized the preparation of a completely new set of plans, known as Structure and Local Plans. A Structure Plan is a broad planning strategy for the local authority area consisting of a statement of general planning objectives. A Local Plan is much more specifically related to controlling development, consisting of a map of preferred land use for each part of the local authority area. For both these plans local authorities were required to consult fully with the public. However, because of the time taken to prepare plans and consult properly with the public, there is hardly a local authority in the country that has a statutory approved plan.

Some planning authorities are forced to fall back on plans drawn up in the 1950s and 1960s. In London for example, the only statutory plan is the 1963 revision to the 1951 Initial Development Plan for London. Other authorities are using their own general strategy plans which have been drawn up without full public participation and have no statutory status. Many authorities use a combination of the two, plus draft versions of the Structure Plans. The result is that there is only a very shaky legal basis for planning throughout the country.

All of this is made worse by the nature of the plans themselves. Land-use groupings used by planners are extraordinarily vague. Broad categories such as 'industry', 'residential', 'shops', or 'commercial', each cover a multitude of different uses, many of which have totally different and even opposing social connotations. Thus, housing could include council housing, luxury flats, town houses or hostels for the homeless. Industry could include everything from a high-rent warehouse to an obsolete factory unit. The result of this vague grouping is that many changes in the use of building do not require planning permission from the local authority. For example, one does not have to seek permission to turn a corner grocer shop into an antique shop, nor to convert low rent flats into luxury housing, nor does one need permission to convert cheap office accommodation into office suites for foreign banks. In these cases, permission would be required to alter the outside structure of the buildings but not for the most important social and economic fact, the change of use. This illustrates the prevailing concern of the planning system with physical changes in the environment rather than social or economic changes.

Such limitations are naturally exploited by private developers. A striking instance of this can be seen in Southwark. On one particular site close to an area that is becoming gradually taken over by office development, Richard Seifert on behalf of the British Land property group obtained permission for 'a warehouse' building in an area zoned for light industry. This building is described in the estate agent's brochure as 'a new prestige building: 35,000 sq. ft with extensive car parking, full central heating and high speed lifts to all floors'. There are no loading bays and the ground floor has been prepared to accommodate a computer. The building, a warehouse within the planning regulations, yet easily refurbished, has not yet been let, but it is perfectly legal and no doubt Southwark Council will be under pressure to allow office uses in the building before long.

This example reveals the most important weakness in the planning system. The control of development takes place with reference to maps which contain broad land-use categories but these, along with physical appearance are the only important criteria of planning control. Almost all other considerations are not strictly speaking within the terms of reference of planning legislation. Thus, planning legislation offers few powers with which to create social plans or to implement social policy. For example, planners cannot insist that low-income housing be built on land zoned for housing, or that industrial developments or office buildings are let at low rents. All questions of price or rent are outside the scope of planning.

Equally, planning legislation though taking into account the physical effect of a building on the surrounding area (daylighting, density, and conservation controls etc.) does not take into account the general economic or social consequences of allowing a particular development. There are certain exceptions to this such as when a factory is polluting the air. The implications are very serious, because it is not possible for a scheme to be refused because for example it will push up land values or will increase the number of homeless or will cause prices to rise in the local shops. Even the argument that a development will set a precedent for further applications of the same type and start an undesirable trend is ruled out according to a judgment made in the High Court. This does not mean that such views are not expressed in the planning arena, but they cannot be used to oppose a planning decision in a court of law.

We have said in the previous chapters that developers judge schemes on the basis of financial criteria, and one might hope that planners could do the same. But this is not allowed in planning law. For instance, a planning authority cannot turn down a scheme which meets all the usual planning criteria but gives inadequate planning benefit to the community, in the form of, say, housing or a cash payment or a row of shops. Thus, there is no incentive for the planning system to examine the financial side of a development deal and no need whatever for the property market to offer to the local authority any financial assessment of the scheme. It follows that any discussions of the developers' profit is not allowed, and local authorities cannot turn a scheme down because it constitutes speculation or is a waste of resources.

The developer is, therefore, in a very strong position compared with the planners or the public. He need only justify his proposals in pure physical planning terms. In addition, he will have employed a team of surveyors, and valuers and ex-local authority planners who are experts at presenting their schemes to planners and councillors. The team will probably know the local area at least as well and probably better than the local authority planners, especially with the high turnover of planners in Inner London, and most large developers employ surveyors and property consultants who are experienced at dealing with the particular local authority in which the development is located. These people often know more about the workings of the local planning department and are more familiar with the thinking of the chief borough planners than anyone else inside or outside the planning department.

The developer's team also probably knows more about planning than the planners. It knows the local planning situation backwards because it has dealt with it so many times and of course knows how to squeeze the maximum amount of profitable space out of a development site. Oliver Marriott in his book, *The Property Boom*, describes how Richard Seifert acting for Harry Hyams of Oldham Estates was able to pack office space onto sites in ways that amazed the planners at the London County Council (LCC), largely because he knew the laws intimately and was able to take full advantage of them. The LCC thought that the traffic circle they persuaded Hyams to construct underneath Centre Point was a reasonable planning benefit. For Hyams is was unbelievably little to ask in return for the potential profit on Centre Point itself.

The developer is still in a strong position even if the local authority turns down his proposal. He has the right to appeal immediately to the Secretary of State for the Environment to ask for his case to be heard by an inspector from the Department of the Environment. If he wins, neither the local authority nor the public have any right to appeal. Indeed, the local authority may have to defend its own decision at the ratepayers' expense at a public inquiry called on behalf of a developer. It goes without saying that at such an inquiry the arguments are conducted on physical planning grounds which usually suit the developer perfectly.

Quite obviously the local authority is in a weak position in the bargaining process over development schemes, but what about the public? The general public is supposed to be informed and safeguarded through the procedures that exist for public consultation. Local authorities have a statutory obligation to consult with the public during the preparation of Structure and Local Plans and are obliged to inform the public about all planning applications, changes in the road system, use of compulsory purchase orders, and must also consult on other matters such as the designation of housing action areas, conservation areas, and listed buildings. In theory then, the public is entitled to be informed and involved in practically every decision a local planning authority has to take. Why is it, therefore, that public participation is usually inadequate?

One of the most important reasons for this is that from the point of view of the developers public consultation, involving as it does delay and disclosure, damages the profitability of projects.

This is particularly likely during a period of inflation when costs are rising sharply all the time. The general attitude of the property world is summarized below in two typical quotes. A surveyor acting for the Norwich Union Company said in 1973:

One thing I think we shall all be spared is planning control by the public. Let us hope that there will not be a proliferation of exhibitions of new projects on which the public are invited to air their views. What a futile waste of time I suggest this can be.

And a developer, quoted in the *Evening Standard* of 24 May 1973 said:

Too many schemes have been fouled up in the past when the public hears about them.

It is thus in the interest of the developer to keep the details of his scheme as secret as possible and to get it through the planning authority with the minimum of contact with the public. There is of course no obligation on the part of the developer to present his proposals to the public and anyhow discussions with planners and councillors in the local authority are often much easier than attempting to consult with the public.

Unfortunately, most local authorities do not go out of their way to compensate for the secrecy of the developers. There is a general reluctance to consult in depth with the public because it seems to the planners and councillors to be such a time-consuming process. There is as well often mistrust of 'the motives' of those who become involved in public consultation exercises. Local authorities are especially suspicious of community organizations and action groups and are rarely prepared to tap the vast store of knowledge in these organizations. This is even acknowledged by the planning establishment. For example, the Town and Country Planning Association remarked in a report on public participation published in June 1974 that

The majority of planning officers are quite unwilling to establish working relationships with local activist groups and both planning officers and councillors frequently hold unwarrantedly jaundiced views of the value of community action in planning terms.

In addition, planning legislation does not encourage proper consultation. In spite of the references to consultation in the planning acts and in circulars from the Department of the Environment, very little time is allowed for consultation particularly over planning applications. The law says that the public has twenty days to respond to planning applications. Yet since it takes at least three months to conduct an effective information and consultation campaign with the public on a development scheme and much longer on large or complex proposals, this time limit is clearly in conflict with the spirit of the acts. If planning authorities decide to take a long time considering a scheme, the applicant is quite entitled to appeal to the Secretary of State for the Environment on the grounds of unreasonable delay. Consequently, from the point of view of both the developer and the planning authority there is much to be gained by discussing the scheme behind closed doors before it reaches the planning application stage. When the application is finally submitted any public consultation is just a formality.

These difficulties and contradictions about public participation have now become so obvious that the government is considering ways of altering the process by which planning applications are considered. In 1973 the Conservative government commissioned a review of the development control system under the chairmanship of a planning lawyer named George Dobry. Much of the pressure for this review came from developers and from the Department of the Environment both of whom were worried by the huge backlog of planning applications and appeals generated by the property boom. They were particularly concerned about delays on large schemes. The final report of the Dobry Commission came out early in 1975 and although the circumstances under which the review was commissioned had changed, the report was seen by many as a non-partisan assessment containing recommendations on which all political parties would probably agree.

However, the major recommendations of the Dobry report do not point to greater public participation but rather a speed-up in the consideration of all types of planning applications. Dobry proposed that applications should be divided into two classes. Class A classifications representing about 70% of all applications, would cover all minor development and changes of use. These would be processed by local authorities with the minimum of formality and would be deemed granted if the applicant heard nothing from the local authority within forty-two days. Class B applications, those that were more controversial or complex, would be decided within fifty-six days unless the local authority thought that an impact study was necessary, in which case it would have up to six months. It is these larger applications which are of most importance to the development industry and if local authorities are required to meet such a timetable developers will score a minor but significant victory at the expense of public participation. The trend, therefore, after the furore about public involvement in planning in the late 1960s and during the property boom, is for greater streamlining in the planning system. Inevitably, this means more public relations and less serious participation.

In this brief review of the most important elements of the present planning system, we have indicated that the main beneficiaries of the system are not the public or the local authorities but the development industry. Indeed, the planning system is largely organized around the demands and pressures of developers and their professional advisers. But more important is the irony that the work that local authorities put into structure plans and development control so inhibits the supply of development sites in certain areas that land values and rents are forced to rise. Thus, the main effect of planning in areas of high demand for property such as the south-east is to protect the value of land and property and consequently to maintain a healthy property investment market.

Local authorities are placed in an appalling dilemma. If they encourage private development where demand has built up, say on suburban housing sites or on sites close to city centres, they can be accused of triggering huge bonanzas for developers. If they refuse to allow development they may be accused of causing dereliction and planning blight and of causing values to rise elsewhere. On the other hand, local authorities benefit from the *status quo* since they welcome the rise in rateable values that comes from high land and property values. Such a delicate situation hardly invites pressure for change from within the planning system and it is therefore only during the exceptional circumstances of spectacular boom or dire slump that there is any move to alter the rules of the game.

The Development Powers of Local Authorities

We have concentrated on the process of development control because it is the principal function of the planning system. But in addition, we must examine the powers that exist to allow local authorities and the central government to develop property and land on their own initiative. These powers can in fact, be called upon only in rather exceptional circumstances but they are important as the background to the Labour Party's thinking about extending the involvement of local authorities in commercial development.

The most important of these exceptions is the development procedure for the new towns. Under the New Towns Act of 1965, new-town corporations have powers to acquire land and to undertake developments of all kinds including commercial schemes such as offices, shopping centres, and factories. They can finance these schemes on their own or they can participate with a financial institution or a developer and of course they can retain the profits themselves.

Other local authorities (except in London) have for some time been able to participate with developers in town centre redevelopment schemes if they own at least part of the land. This was first actively encouraged by the 1944 Town and Country Planning Act which allowed local authorities to go into partnership with developers in the redevelopment of bombed-out city centres. The usual practice was for the local authority to acquire the land and to grant ninety-nine-year leases to developers at a fixed ground rent. In this way, the centres of Exeter, Plymouth, Bristol, Coventry, Portsmouth, and Southampton, and many other cities were rebuilt. Later similar arrangements spread to town centres all over the country.

The original formula for participation proved to be much more profitable for the developers than for the local authorities. This was because the developer was free to review the rents charged to tenants of his buildings on a regular basis while the local authority was stuck with a ground rent which was fixed and usually absurdly low. Thus, in later schemes, ground rents were also reviewed on a regular basis and were set at a percentage of the rents received by the developer.

Other forms of partnership with developers are possible under existing law. For example, according to Section 52 of the 1971 Town and Country Planning Act local authorities are entitled to enter into agreements with landowners to cover the costs of providing essential services to a development. There are examples, too, of joint companies formed between developers and local authorities. In 1971 the Norwich City Council acquired a three-acre site near the city centre and rather than granting a long lease to a development company, it decided to set up a joint development company called Colegate Development Limited. Each partner holds 50% of the shares and the arrangement is that the company undertakes the development and both partners share in the profits. Short-term finance is supplied by a bank and long-term finance by an insurance company. Another example of a local authority development company is the Buckingham Borough Development Company Limited, incorporated in 1971. This company will buy unserviced land from landowners which will then be supplied with services and sold to development companies for housing. The company and the landowners will split the profits.

There have also been suggestions that redevelopment could be undertaken by non-profit-making companies working closely with local authorities. We saw in Chapter 1 how in 1973 a development company, Stock Conversion Ltd., stood to make £20 million or more from the redevelopment of Tolmers Square. As an alternative two property journalists, Christopher Booker and Bennie Gray, formed a company called Claudius Properties which they claimed could carry out the development on terms that would return much greater benefit to Camden Council. Stock Conversion had offered to share part of the site with the Council if Camden would agree to serve Compulsory Purchase Orders (CPOs) on those pieces of land not yet acquired by the company and if permission were granted for a large office development which, as we have seen, would be worth £35 million or more. Claudius made a counter offer which would have provided most of the site free of charge to the Council in return for granting consent for a smaller office development, the size of which would have been just sufficient to cover the costs of buying the site and building the office block. In other words the office development would be non-profit-making and Camden would acquire some free land. In order to carry out the scheme, it would be necessary to persuade the Secretary of State for the Environment to approve compulsory purchase orders on all the land including that already in the ownership of Stock Conversion. This proposal stirred up immense controversy in the press and such was the pressure on Camden Council that it turned down the Stock Conversion scheme and promised to investigate the Claudius proposal. But the Council was not convinced that the Secretary of State would allow the CPOs and doubted whether such an untried scheme would be financed by the banks.

In any case, these questions were never answered because of the sudden collapse of the property market in 1974, and the situation has not yet been resolved. It may be that such schemes are not feasible outside a period of exceptional profitability for office development but the economic principle behind the scheme seems sound. Local authorities are, however, likely to be suspicious of untried approaches and will favour schemes which involve them in the minimum amount of risk. This is why local authorities are not usually prepared to entertain such ideas seriously as long as private developers are prepared to go ahead without any local authority effort or financial involvement. And to be fair to local authorities, with costs of land and building running at unprecedented levels, the financial commitment might be enormous. In a pure market situation, there is little incentive for local authorities or central government to get involved unless they have special privileges.

The most important powers that local authorities need in order to stimulate involvement in development schemes are powers to buy land cheaply and borrow money at low rates of interest. Both of these powers have been forbidden to local authorities for many years. Under the 1961 Land Compensation Act local authorities were required to pay the market value for land whether or not a CPO was involved. There were certain exceptions to this rule but they were so restricting that almost no effective use was made of them. For example, the Act said that local authorities would not have to pay that part of the value of a site which was created by the 'hope value' of development but that this discount would not apply where land values had risen due to the publication of the general strategy plan for the area. This was obviously absurd since all local authorities have a duty to produce plans to guide development. In practice then, the 1961 Land Compensation Act virtually prohibited local authority development initiatives, since the costs of land forms such a large part of the total cost of development.

Local authorities also need access to cheap money or government grants if they are to initiate development schemes. But again they are in a very weak position. Local authority borrowing is divided into 'key sector' expenditure and 'locally determined schemes'. Key sector money is finance provided for services for which policy is determined by central government, such as education, housing, water supply and major roads. It could not be used for buying land in city centres unless this was part of the normal local authority housing programme and even if such an argument was made the Department of the Environment would still have to sanction individual projects and doubtless would need to be convinced that this money could not be better spent on some other aspect of the housing programme. It is undeniable that large amounts of money can buy only small amounts of land in central areas whereas the same amount could purchase more elsewhere. This is how the idea of 'central area uses' on privately owned land has been perpetuated.

Money for locally determined schemes is usually less than key sector money and is given in the form of a block allocation which can be spent in any way local authorities wish. For most local authorities, the purchase of high-value land and buildings would be a low priority for the use of such loans. If they wished to spend large amounts on land assembly local authorities would almost certainly have to borrow from other sources although this too would require statutory authorization.

After the war almost all local authority borrowing was from the Public Works Loan Board (PWLB) which lent money from the Exchequer at rates of interest which were below the rates prevailing in the money markets. But in 1955 the Conservative government imposed severe restrictions on PWLB loans and forced local authorities to borrow money from the market at the going rate of interest. Consequently, whereas in 1951, 85% of local authority borrowing was from PWLB, by 1960 this had shrunk to about 10%, much to the benefit of the discount houses and foreign finance houses which lent the balance.

Money is in such short supply that it is not surprising to find that in most local authority budgets money for land purchase and commercial development makes little impact within the local authority area. For example, the total capital budget for 1974–5 for the Greater London Council is £395 million of which £330 million will be borrowed from the money markets at the going rate. About £6 million of this will be allocated to land assembly in GLC Comprehensive Development Areas. Most of these areas are in central London where land values are incredibly high and it is thus doubtful whether £6 million could buy more than three or four acres of land in Covent Garden, just one of the Comprehensive Development Areas over which the GLC wants to exert some influence. Therefore, one cannot escape the conclusion that controlling development is a low priority for the GLC, and other local authorities under the present land legislation.

The Development Powers of Central Government

Central government is the largest single user of office space in the country and yet it has no more powers to undertake commercial development than local authorities. Though the government has always owned and managed land and property it was not until 1972 that an agency was formed to look after the state's property interests. This agency is called the Property Services Agency (PSA) and it is noteworthy that it was established by the Conservative government to introduce a more business-like approach into the government's property activities. The PSA is the custodian of 17,661 acres of land, excluding 607,000 acres at the disposal of the Ministry of Defence, and it manages a massive 105 million sq. ft of property of all kinds.

One of the main aims of the PSA was to try to reduce the government's enormous and rapidly rising rent bill. Most civil servants are accommodated in office space that is rented by the government at normal market rents, and of the total 32.8 million sq. ft, 4.3 million is in London where of course, rents are the highest in the country. For London alone, the government paid out £41 million in rents in 1974 and estimates from the PSA indicate that this could rise to £125 million by 1984 as a number of long leases fall due and as rents in London continue their steady climb. There is one way out of this situation and that is for the PSA to develop properties for government departments.

But the Conservative government was naturally reluctant to give the PSA powers to do this on any significant scale because of the implications it would have for the dozens of property companies and financial institutions who receive the government's rent roll. Thus, the PSA has very restricted powers to buy land or borrow money and the only large scheme that has got near the planning stage is the Vauxhall Effra project near Vauxhall Bridge which, if built, could accommodate 7,000 civil servants. The Labour government faced with the same pressures as the Conservatives and striving to cut public expenditure as well, have done nothing to change this situation.

Similar restrictions apply to other state agencies such as British Rail and the Gas Board. British Rail since 1969 has managed its property interests through the British Rail Property Board. It cannot develop its own sites but must go into partnership with developers and it is clearly in the interests of the property world that this should continue. The Peachey Property Corporation which has undertaken many station redevelopment schemes with British Rail has been one of the main beneficiaries of this policy (see Chapter 5).

Interventions by the Government

The measures that the property world fear most are not those connected with the general planning process or even those that involve changes in the planning acts, but those that hit at the financial basis of their operations, that affect investment and profitability. And the measures they most welcome are those that make it easier to undertake profitable developments.

These measures cover a wide range of government policy –

rent controls, taxation of development gains, changes in the law of compensation for compulsory purchase, land hoarding charges, the financial provisions of local authority/developer partnership schemes, the public ownership of development land, and many more. In contrast with changes in planning law most of these controls can be introduced rapidly because they can be incorporated in budget statements or finance bills but they are undoubtedly more political than changes in the procedures for development control. Since they are introduced at one moment and withdrawn at the next, they create uncertainty in the property market and are thus the special target of criticism by the property industry.

Probably the most important measure of all is the legislation governing commercial rents. Commercial rent control was first introduced under the Conservative counter-inflation policy and although it exempted new buildings, it produced a sustained uproar from the property world, usually the friend of Conservative governments. In the end, the enormous lobby for property which included all the major banks and institutions as well as the developers, convinced the Conservatives in October 1973 that 'long-term control of business rents was neither practicable nor desirable'. This great victory for the property market went unchallenged by the Labour government when they came into office in March 1974 in spite of many fierce attacks on property while Labour was in opposition. Labour's decision was made for exactly the same reason as the Conservatives'; they feared the implications for the banking and property system of a prolonged freeze on business rents. During a time in which income from normal commercial activity was declining it was immensely reassuring to the business world that income could still be obtained from property. Also, of course, the property investment market was dead without steadily rising rents.

The taxation of development gains is another controversial form of government intervention. Even the most enthusiastic supporters of a free market in property development acknowledge that the planning system makes it possible for landowners and developers to pick up windfall gains from local authority planning decisions. Consequently, successive Labour governments have sought to find a formula for taxing these increases in value. Labour came up with various proposals in 1947 and again in 1964 but none of these survived, largely because the property market refused to cooperate. Developers and landowners were naturally reluctant to undertake developments or sell land when they knew they would be heavily taxed. And this remains the problem once again in 1975 with developers facing a proposed 80% tax on development gains. In other words, developers or landowners (when the tax comes into effect) will have to pay 80% of the difference between the value of a site before hope of development and the value with development. But the effectiveness of this tax like its predecessors will depend on whether the property market will simply sit it out until the Conservatives are returned. The answer to this dilemma lies in much more radical interventions than any the present Labour government are contemplating. These we shall discuss in Chapter 7.

Though not affecting the way in which profits are calculated, government policies towards the location of office and industrial development can also have dramatic effects on the profitability of development in different parts of the country. We have already seen in the last chapter that property investors put most of their money into London and the south-east because it is there that demand for property has remained at high levels for many years and where rents are highest. How do government policies towards the location of offices and industry effect this pattern?

In 1965 the Labour government introduced legislation called the Control of Office and Industrial Development Act with the aim of encouraging new development and new employment opportunities in the regions instead of in the south-east. Under the Act, developers were required to obtain an Office Development Permit (ODP) before applying for planning permission from a local authority. Initially, any office building of more than 3,000 sq. ft, in the south-east required an ODP but later the limit was raised to 10,000 sq. ft. In order for a developer to get an ODP he had to show that the firm that was to occupy the proposed building really needed to be in London or the south-east. The idea was to force all other firms to the regions.

For the first three years of the Act, office and industrial development in London was cut back sharply and there was some move by developers to other regions. But growth was transferred to the periphery of the south-east and to the Midlands instead of those areas of the country that needed it most, and so the legislation was extended to include both the west and the east Midlands. Even this extension did not benefit areas such as the north-east and Scotland very much because office development tended to go to relatively prosperous places like Bristol which were not covered by the restrictions.

One of the most dramatic results of the Act and the one that underlined the basic difficulties with this type of control, was the way in which development restrictions in the south-east and the Midlands reinforced the boom of rents and property values. Rents for new office space in the City of London rose from an average of £5 per sq. ft in 1967 to £10 per sq. ft in 1971 and £20 per sq. ft in 1973. In other words, London and the south-east became more attractive places for property investment as a result of the Act rather than less. In fact, so obvious did this become that ODP restrictions were significantly relaxed after 1969, but since by that time the demand for office space in the south-east easily outstripped supply in spite of the relaxation of controls, rents kept rising.

The attitude of the property and financial world to all this was rather ambivalent. Though developers and financial interests were the main beneficiaries of the rise in values caused by the restrictions on the supply of office space, the property market has always publicly opposed interference in the free market in land and property. Also the City's Committee on Invisible Exports has attacked ODP restrictions because it claims that the provision of office space in Central London is essential to the continued growth of invisible exports and that Britain's position as a financial centre will be threatened if financial institutions cannot locate or expand in Central London.

Yet ODP restrictions are still actively used by the government. In December 1973, the Conservatives went as far as placing a freeze on all ODPs in the south-east, and this policy was continued by the succeeding Labour government. It is important to note however that many local authorities, even Labour controlled ones, do not support such restrictions because they are often in conflict with their own development plans. The GLC for example, wants office development to be directed to suburban centres such as Croydon and Lewisham but ODP policy has not really discriminated very much between different areas of the south-east. In a similar way, ODP policy has not been concerned with the distribution of development within other regions of the country. A new office building in the north-east for example probably means an office in central Newcastle rather than in other parts of the region where office employment might be needed.

Many of the same arguments can be made about Industrial Development Certificates which were first introduced in 1948. The main effect of IDC policy appears to have been to accelerate the drift of industrial firms away from the south-east, but rather than bringing benefits to the depressed regions or those parts of the regions that have the worst problems, it has encouraged the further growth of areas such as the Midlands and areas on the periphery of the south-east. In other words, industrial development has gone to those areas that benefited most from the ODP policy. And just as ODPs have caused office rents to rise in the south-east so IDCs have caused industrial rents to rise in the south-east. This side-effect, in itself, is sufficient to deter some industrial firms from locating there.

Overall, the ODP and IDC approach to the problem of development and property investment represents a classic planning strategy. It assumes that the government can manipulate office rents, or the distribution of employment, or the costs and benefits of development, by the geographical distribution of offices and industrial premises. But by attempting this, the government has simply provided yet another stimulus to finance capital and the property market. It often seems that governments persist with ODPs and IDCs because they do not wish to face up to the need for more fundamental changes.

Conclusions

The state intervenes in the property market through the planning system and through the introduction of various financial measures. Of these two roles, planning is by far the least controversial from the point of view of the finance and property world and to a large extent benefits the property market by restricting the number and distribution of development sites. It follows from this that the normal reforms of planning legislation such as procedures for drawing up plans and considering planning applications are of little consequence to the property market. Often these changes work to its advantage. In contrast, local authorities and the general public, especially those who suffer from redevelopment, are in a weak and often very vulnerable position even though it is they who draw up development plans and give partial or complete approval to them.

Much more threatening to the property world but not always of benefit to local authorities or the public are various government measures aimed at regulating the cycles of booms and slumps in the property market. Historically, the purpose of rent controls and taxation of development values has been to check over-investment in property during a boom. When the market begins to slump these restrictions are removed and incentives may be introduced in order to stimulate investment. But even as responses to market fluctuations, they are easily attacked because they are applied too late or because they have unfair side-effects, and because they do not solve the basic problems of making land available for housing and industry in the areas in which there is the greatest social need. Consequently, these interventions are not aimed at changing the basis of the property market.

Chapter 4

The Impact of the System on
North Southwark

> Area — 38½ acres. Value — £300 million plus . . .
> This is the magnitude of the plan to redevelop Hays
> Wharf — a plan for the largest and most exciting com-
> mercial project to be undertaken in London since the
> Great Fire of 1666.
>
> October 1971. The Proprietors of Hays Wharf, *City
> within a City*, Document circulated to shareholders

> After the annual meeting, Sir David Burnett [of Hays
> Wharf] said that Southwark Council's approval of the
> revised Strategy Plan for Thames-side redevelopment
> had slightly altered the draft strategy by reducing the
> office content, but it still gave Hays Wharf what it had
> always planned for.
>
> *Financial Times*, 25 January 1974

Ten years ago, commuters passing through North Southwark on
their way to main line stations at London Bridge, Cannon Street,
or Charing Cross would scarcely have looked up from their newspapers as they passed through the densely packed district of factories, wharves, warehouses, and tenements on the south bank of
the Thames. Unattractive, grimy, off the beaten track, no place to
find an office job or a businessman's flat, yet unmistakably within
a stone's throw of St Paul's and the City of London.

Ten years later a remarkable transformation has taken place.
North Southwark is on the map — an extension of the City and
the West End. Office towers dominate the skyline. In all direc-
tions historic buildings are being gutted and converted into prestige office suites. Derelict land and scaffolding are evident every-
where. Guided tours take in the area. North Southwark has been
discovered. Most important of all, it has been discovered by the
commercial property market and the planners, valuers, and councillors of the Labour dominated London Borough of Southwark.

The causes of this transformation and its costs and benefits are
the subject of this chapter. Though it might seem to be an ex-

treme case with which to illustrate the effects of the property boom on a working community, it is quite apparent from the ravages created by redevelopment elsewhere in London and other large cities that the Southwark experience is very far from unique. The list of parallels in London is endless and reads like a package tour of 'old London' – Covent Garden, Wapping High Street, Piccadilly Circus, Soho, Battersea Riverside, Holborn and Bermondsey. What these places have in common is a central location with potentially exploding land values and a predominantly commercial or industrial character. What has happened to these areas and North Southwark in particular illustrates the power of financial values over the jobs and homes of working-class Londoners.

The character of North Southwark

North Southwark stretches along the south bank of the Thames from Blackfriars Bridge to Tower Bridge with a hinterland reaching back about a mile to the Elephant and Castle. Along the riverside and in large blocks behind are warehouses, factories, derelict wharves, and hundreds of small firms under the railway arches carrying the main lines to the commuter termini.

Almost half of the workers in the factories and warehouses used to live locally in nineteenth-century tenements. It was convenient for industrial firms then and indeed until after the war, for their workers to live close to work. But over the last twenty years and particularly over the last ten years, the population has fallen steadily from over 40,000 in 1961 to about 26,000 in 1974. The bulk of this loss has been due to the Council policy of slum clearance combined with rehousing away from the area. The modernization of flats and general decline in family size has had its effect too. In fact, it is now Council policy to discourage further family accommodation in the area. Nevertheless, over 30% of the population still live in private blocks of flats owned by the Peabody Trust, the Guinness Trust or the Church Commissioners, while almost all of the others live in Council flats. Less than 1% are owner-occupiers.

The population is overwhelmingly working class with nearly 60% of the heads of households in manual industrial jobs compared with 45% for London as a whole. Many wives go out to work, some doing secretarial work, others factory work or office cleaning. An increasing percentage of the population, nearly 18%, are old age pensioners. Most families have been in or near the area for at least two generations. Part of North Southwark lies in the old Borough of Bermondsey (now merged with the old Borough of Southwark) and in this area where there are more Council flats, people are solidly Labour though the voting turn-out for local elections is quite low. Further east in the private trust accommodation, there is less active Labour Party allegiance and voter turnouts are the lowest in the borough.

Residents have always been short of the amenities enjoyed by the wealthier and newer parts of London. Play space and open space provision are well below the accepted planning standards. One Council report describes the environment in the following way:

Generally, environmental conditions within the housing areas are poor. There are deficiencies in playspace, amenity space, off-street parking, and garaging and community facilities like tenants' halls. The design and layout of the housing offers little scope for improvement in its present form. Blocks of housing are built around surfaced yards, now used for car parking, or in the case of tenements, extremely confined in space.

However, prior to the property boom, the area was not short of pubs and social clubs and at one time there was a cinema and a swimming pool. But many of these facilities have long since gone, and, as slum clearance has progressed, many housing estates stand isolated and cut off among the factories, office buildings, and busy main roads. As we shall see later on, Southwark Council's plans for the area have been partly responsible for the decline in facilities for the residents.

An important key to understanding the changes that have swept through North Southwark over the last ten years is the industrial structure. Many of London's traditional industries, such as printing, engineering, food and drink trades, and transport have been heavily concentrated in Southwark and Bermondsey. Some were tied to the docks, such as food importing, others such as printing to the City of London, and others such as printing engineers to other firms in the area. Some of the country's best-known firms had headquarters in the area, Sainsbury, Crosse and Blackwell, Courage, for example. Both the Borough fruit and vegetable market and the Leathermarket were located in the area. On the riverside, stretching from London Bridge to Tower Bridge along Tooley Street, lay 'the larder of England' – the wharves and warehouses of one of the oldest wharfage firms in London, the Proprietors of Hays Wharf.

Thousands of workers were needed to serve these firms for decades until the early 1960s. Beginning slowly but picking up tremendous momentum by 1970, firms of all descriptions began to lay off workers, close down or move out. A host of economic factors can be used to explain these events, including mergers, moves to larger premises, closure of archaic businesses, loss of trade, and the loss of firms in related trades. But a vital trigger mechanism, and the process that compressed the collapse of industry into such a short period, was the unprecedented boom in land values starting in 1963 and reaching a peak in 1973.

Hays Wharf

Nothing illustrates the recent history of the area better than the activities of one particularly ambitious firm, Hays Wharf. This company has been in existence since the eighteenth century, controlling one of London's most important wharves with a key position next to London Bridge, facing the City.

Under the shrewd guidance of one of its directors, a chartered surveyor, Sir David Burnett, the company began to acquire land in the 1950s all along Southwark's riverside until, by 1965, the company held the freehold of thirty-eight acres of wharves and warehouses between London Bridge and Tower Bridge, along what is known as Tooley Street. Meanwhile, the company built a series of wharves and cold-storage depots much further down river away from the troublesome and expensive Dock Labour Board area, thus freeing their entire Tooley Street operation for land speculation and eventual redevelopment.

The effect on jobs was shattering. In September 1968, the company employed 5,379 people, of which 2,000 were registered dock workers, but by 1970 the total number of employees had fallen by over 2,000. The Tooley Street wharves were closed. Several present-day Southwark councillors and the local MP were themselves made redundant.

Any thought that the closure of the wharves was due to a sudden arrival of containerization methods or an outbreak of strikes, was dispelled during the next few months as the shares of Hays Wharf rose from 154p in June 1970 to 402p in January 1971 on the rumours of plans for the redevelopment of Hays Wharf. In February 1971, the *Economist* carried a leader on the firm predicting that there would be 1.5 million sq. ft of office space on the site.

These rumours proved to be extremely well founded because in April 1971, the London Borough of Southwark published their plans for North Southwark which changed the land use of Hays Wharf from 'Waterside Uses' to 'West End Uses'. But the boldness of Hays Wharf's vision did not become public knowledge until October 1971. On 26 October, the company circulated to its shareholders, and launched with great fanfare at a Press Conference, a glossy document prepared by Sir William Holford and Partners, and called *City within a City*. This document heralded 'the most exciting commercial project to be undertaken in London since the Great Fire of 1666'. *The Times* described the plan as

... a new West End south of the river with shops, restaurants, public houses, tourist attractions, and homes, as well as offices and hotels; that is the effect of the masterplan published today for threequarters of a mile of down-at-heel warehouse land ... the total value of the plan is estimated at over £300 million.

The Strategy Plan for Thames-side

The plan that turned Hays Wharf into a property company and gave the go-ahead for redevelopment of much of North Southwark was called the *Strategy Plan for Southwark's Thames-side*. It might appear mystifying that such a plan should have been launched by an all-Labour Borough at a time when public opinion was rounding on property speculators and wholesale re-development. An examination of the history and circumstances behind the plan suggest that what happened was in fact all too familiar, though the geographical and financial scale of it all was exceptional.

Under the Initial Development Plan (IDP) for London and its revised version in 1962, most of North Southwark was zoned for residential or for 'Waterside and Industrial Uses'. Such office development as there was was concentrated in what is known as the South Bank Comprehensive Development Area (CDA). The South Bank CDA came into being in the 1955 IDP but was conceived much earlier by Abercombie in his 1943 Plan for London. Abercombie, and the planners who drew up the IDP, held the view that the South Bank of the Thames was a dirty and run-down area and an unworthy neighbour to the north side of the river with its Embankment and new office buildings. They, therefore, designated a great sweep of riverside from Vauxhall to Waterloo Bridge as an area in which redevelopment would take place on a comprehensive basis, and in which office development would be permitted. This area was later extended further east-wards and discussion centred around whether the CDA should go still further downstream as far as London Bridge, that is, as far as Hays Wharf.

Consequently, some offices were built in the 1950s and early 1960s in North Southwark. By far the largest was the building in Southwark Street, developed by Charles Clore's Centre City Properties and occupied by the Ministry of Transport. Clore was particularly proud of this building; not because of its design but because of its size, location, the speed with which it was built, and the quality of the tenant. Elsewhere in North Southwark, there were few offices except those attached to industrial concerns and import-export companies.

Apart from discussions about extending the CDA, the first clear indications that the planners and politicians wanted exten-sive redevelopment of Thames-side came with the preparation of the Greater London Development Plan (GLDP). The GLDP was intended to replace the outdated IDP and constituted one of the first major strategic tasks for the Greater London Council which replaced the London County Council in 1965. Throughout the preparation of the GLDP, the Greater London Council was under the control of the Conservatives and one might have expected a good deal of controversy between Labour Boroughs and the GLC planners over planning policy.

In the case of Southwark this was not so. GLC and Southwark planners and politicians reached agreement early on that North Southwark should be re-zoned for office and hotel development, and thus when Southwark submitted its official comments on the draft GLDP, there was no reference at all to the re-zoning of North Southwark or indeed to GLC office policy. If the GLDP had been approved quickly there might have been no need for the Strategy Plan. But the prolonged inquiry into the GLDP made Southwark impatient.

There were special reasons why Southwark could not wait. One of these was that Hays Wharf had shut down its Tooley Street wharves and was pressing Southwark for a decision about redevelopment. The second reason, which in retrospect seems remarkable, was that Southwark planners were getting alarmed by dereliction and 'planning blight' and were afraid that much of North Southwark would lie derelict for years unless the developers were given strong encouragement to move in. Indeed, some felt that Southwark would miss out completely on the office boom. The Southwark Public Relations office churned out leaflets for developers and industrialists heralding the opportunities in Thames-side. For example, one leaflet talked of '150 acres of land ready for IMMEDIATE redevelopment. Owners of land and developers are "talking turkey" with prospective clients. Thames-side is wide open for development. Try Southwark. We will put you in contact with owners of land and developers.' The fear was, even at the height of property boom, that not enough developers and land owners would show any interest.

The plan itself was put together in a hurry. It was commissioned in October 1970 with a deadline for the council elections in April 1971. The idea was to identify 'the areas of change' and the areas for potential redevelopment. No consideration whatever was given to social patterns, the effects of the plan or re-zoning on jobs, or to the costs and benefits of the whole strategy. No surveys were undertaken. Some thought was given to how much rate-income would be produced by the offices and the Borough valuers pushed for high plot-ratios so as to get as much office content as possible.

The result was a draft plan for five million sq. ft of offices and a wide open invitation for developers to get on with it. The office content was in fact far in excess of that proposed in the Conservative GLDP written statement. And yet the planners in the absence of any public consultation or reaction were quite pleased with their work. They thought the plan was novel, being an informal strategy, and felt that it might be a sensible control of offices with development being restricted to 'opportunity areas'. No concern was expressed at the absence of social planning; this was not thought to be relevant for this type of plan.

The politicians were also pleased – or at least those who knew about the plan at all. It is quite characteristic for planning schemes to be judged and negotiated by a very small number of people. The first draft of the Strategy Plan was not debated in Council prior to its adoption and had made just one visit to the Planning and Development Committee.

The Council gave two main reasons for wanting the plan. The first was that the Borough was poor and was faced with a declining rate base. Some substitute for the docks and factories in North Southwark was needed. It was estimated at that time that five million sq. ft of office space would yield £5 million a year in rates assuming a modest rate yield of about £1 per sq. ft. Set against a massive capital debt of £120 million, this would be a considerable boost to income and borrowing power. Moreover, many councillors believed that North Southwark was in need of redevelopment and since the Council owned less than 5% of the land, the Borough required the help of private developers.

The Council as a whole and many of the planners had no idea that the document they passed in draft form in April 1971 was controversial. It was felt that Thames-side was a good area for office development and conversely was not a good area for family housing. They regarded the population as small and dwindling and if the residents did not like the plan this was a small price to pay and anyhow, as the Chairman of Planning said in 1972, probably few of those complaining would be living in the area when the plan came to fruition. This was quite inaccurate because most of the population was and still is living in very solid

Council flats and private trust estates. What was really meant, perhaps, was that there was only a small residential population around the areas of greatest redevelopment, that is along the riverside, and many councillors did not realize how redevelopment would affect the hinterland. For example, when one local councillor who had a small shop in the hinterland in Borough High Street was asked how he felt about the Strategy Plan now that his own business was threatened by an application for redevelopment, he remarked that 'the Strategy Plan hasn't reached me yet'.

The other local councillors accepted the draft Strategy Plan with equal good grace. Since there was no public consultation campaign at this stage there was no means of judging public reaction. And the councillors themselves were poorly briefed about the plan because it was not debated in Council nor at ward party meetings. The plan was circulated to councillors in the form of a typically technical planning report written by planning officers as if it were a quite uncontroversial matter. Most councillors, therefore, attached little political significance to the report, preferring to regard it as another planning report 'for discussion' and ultimate decision by the Planning and Development Committee.

It is hardly surprising in view of this sort of presentation that local residents and workers were almost completely unaware of the existence of the Strategy Plan until a year after its publication. But once the word got around, not by a Council consultation exercise, but by local tenants and community associations, a large campaign of opposition to the plan began to develop. Objectors criticized the appalling lack of consultation and the disregard for the needs and wishes of residents and workers in the area. The five million sq. ft of office space initially proposed was attacked as excessive and the planners were accused of encouraging property speculation and causing the closure of factories, corner shops, and warehouses. The mounting wave of criticism spread to the national press and television and, as a result of this storm, approval of the plan was delayed for four months. Revisions to the plan were hastily introduced and promises of consultation 'at every stage in the planning process' were uttered by the Chairman of the Planning Committee. Some important amendments were written into the final draft of the Strategy Plan that went to full Council in November 1973, including the commitment to reserve 75% of all new housing in private developments for the disposal of the Council, but the broad outlines remained the same. The grand switch from Waterside and Industrial Uses to West End Uses stayed as well as the general strategy for redevelopment by the private sector. The policy towards planning gains was tightened up, however, in response to the widespread accusation in the newspapers that Southwark Council was 'giving away' huge profits to developers and land owners.

Though local residents hardly expected Southwark Council to withdraw the Strategy Plan, they hoped that the GLC would intervene since the Labour controlled GLC had been elected in April 1973 on an anti-property developer platform. But they were disappointed. In reply to a question in Council in November 1973 about the revised Strategy Plan, the Chairman of the GLC Planning Committee stated that 'the possibility of 4 million sq. ft of office space in this part of London is strategically unacceptable'. But this strong talk meant very little in practice since three months earlier the very same committee accepted an officer's report containing only mild criticisms of the plan. GLC policy was to prevent an allout conflict with Labour Southwark but to promise local residents that the GLC would take a very critical view of individual applications. But by then considerable damage had been done.

It is possible that the GLC might have taken a stronger line if councillors had been given more encouragement by senior planning officers. Many of these officers had worked with Southwark planners on the GLDP and shared their view that the Strategy Plan was a progressive plan, though at no time had they attempted to find out whether local residents and workers felt the same way. One internal GLC report on the shocking lack of consultation over the plan was never incorporated in the GLC report on the Strategy Plan.

The Department of the Environment was even more ineffective in its protection of local interests. This was to some extent expected since the Conservatives were in power at the time. But it was also due to the peculiar legal status of the Strategy Plan as a 'non-statutory plan'. This meant that the plan was not subject to the same statutory consultation procedures as a Structure or Local Plan and when complaints were made to the Department of the Environment about the preemption of the Local Plan, the reply was characteristically 'write to your local council'.

Another factor taken into account by civil servants at the Department of the Environment was the outcome of a public inquiry back in 1968. This inquiry concerned a large office development proposal for King's Reach on the riverside by Blackfriars Bridge. The application was turned down by Southwark Council on the grounds that the site was zoned for Waterside and Industrial Uses, but the developers appealed and were surprisingly upheld by the Labour Minister of Housing and Local Government. This result convinced many Southwark planners and civil servants at the Department of the Environment that the tide of office development on the Thames-side could not be stemmed. With this sort of analysis, the Strategy Plan made perfect sense.

The Property Developers in North Southwark

If most Southwark councillors, planners and valuers were satisfied with the Strategy Plan, the development industry could hardly believe it. Here was a Labour controlled council welcoming widespread redevelopment of industrial property within a stone's throw of the City of London without demanding substantial planning gains at a time of increasing restriction of office development in Central London by other Labour Boroughs.

Leading estate agents, in their annual reports, labelled Southwark as an outstanding growth area. Office rentals rose to levels equivalent to the West End. But since these rents of £7–8 per sq. ft were still far lower than the City, where new space was letting for £15 per sq. ft, North Southwark became extremely attractive to firms wanting to be close to the City but unwilling to pay City prices.

Well before the Strategy Plan in final form was approved, Southwark Planning Department was deluged with inquiries from developers and land owners. Planning applications began to pour in at a rate of over ten a month for sites in North South-wark and this continued for two years. Very soon there was a huge backlog of applications and dozens of outstanding negotiations between developers and the planners in the development control section. If the Planning Department had been fully staffed a large number of these applications would have been approved. But because of the poor working relations in the department which resulted in a number of resignations many schemes were held up.

Nevertheless, developers and property investors quickly took firm control of North Southwark. The prime sites on the riverside were taken early by the large property giants. Edger Investments bought a huge site close to Blackfriars Bridge and obtained planning permission for the development of an office and computer complex a year before Southwark Council approved the Strategy Plan. Laing Development Company put forward detailed proposals for an office complex on another riverside site before the Plan had even been commissioned. Further along the river, Sterling Guarantee Trust took over Butlers and Colonial Wharves.

On Hays Wharf, three property groups bought development options from the Hays Wharf Company. The St Martins Property Corporation took the area closest to London Bridge, while the remainder of the thirty-eight-acre site was shared between Argyle Securities and Amalgamated Investment and Property. Following the guidelines in the revised Strategy Plan, these companies would be able to develop 1.5 million sq. ft of offices, a 750-room hotel, a shopping centre, and several hundred flats.

In the hinterland, some of the most attractive companies were the traditional industrial firms. For example, Sainsbury, J. Lyons, Courage, and the International Publishing Company (part of Reed International), all owning large sites in North Southwark, established special property divisions to undertake redevelopment of their land holdings. Elsewhere in the hinterland, industrial land was sold to property companies for large sums. Thus, Dalgety acquired the site occupied by an essence works, the Prudential Assurance Company bought the site occupied by a printing firm, the Argyle Securities bought a small engineering firm. In none of the cases quoted was planning permission for office development certain.

Some firms certainly got their fingers burned when the property market collapsed in December 1973. One Croydon-based company called Lawdons Ltd, bought six acres of wharves and warehouses in Bermondsey, only to find that because of planning delays their luxury housing scheme was less and less feasible so that they sold the land to Southwark Council (for £250,000 an acre) at a considerable loss. Another company called Land Use Investments bought a very small site deep in the hinterland for well over £400,000, hoping to trade it again. But the collapse of the property market eliminated this possibility, leaving the company with huge interest payments and an awkward site on which only a small office development could be achieved.

It is also common in an area which has been discovered by the property market to find local estate agents establishing themselves as active developers and buyers of land. One firm called Birrane and Partners is particularly active in North Southwark partly through a development company known as Crowne Freeholds. Mr Birrane wrote in the *Investors Chronicle* in April 1973 that North Southwark was a ghost-town aching to be redeveloped.

Lastly, there are instances of companies which have been formed to undertake just one development in North Southwark. For example, the Fairfield Property Group has farmed out a dozen office developments in Borough High Street to a dozen subsidiary companies, each with the same four directors and shareholders. Since none of these developments exceeds 10,000 sq. ft of office space, no Office Development Permits have been necessary and all of these developments are proceeding on schedule.

Before leaving the developers, mention must be made of the effects of Conservation Areas on the development process in North Southwark. There are two Conservation Areas in the Strategy Plan area, one down Borough High Street and the other on the riverside on the edge of Bermondsey. In Conservation Areas planners discourage demolition and prefer development that is in character with the traditional physical environment. Thus, on Borough High Street, the planners have insisted on buildings of the same height and vaguely similar facade to Borough High Street as it looked in the nineteenth century. But the economics of renovation is such that office or high-priced residential development is practically the only feasible form of redevelopment as far as the developers are concerned. This means that traditional uses whether they are shops, warehouses, or residences over shops have disappeared and Borough High Street is inevitably being transformed into a smart office street with expensive shops. Refurbishing companies such as Haslemere Estates and Compass Securities have made a small fortune out of this type of Conservation area. As with residential Conservation areas, commercial and industrial Conservation areas rapidly lose their character when the developers get to work because traditional tenants are squeezed out. Moreover, purchase by local authorities is ruled out because of the prohibitive costs of acquisition and renovation. Yet the Council is willing to accept these consequences because it is principally interested in preserving the physical character of Conservation Areas rather than their social or functional character.

Impact on the Local Area

Though we have hinted at the widespread impact of redevelopment on North Southwark, we have not described precisely what the impact has been or how it has taken place.

There appear to be three general ways in which redevelopment has affected North Southwark. First of all, the Strategy Plan itself, even without any planning permission being granted, produced an explosion of 'hope values' throughout the area particularly in those places zoned for mixed development or on sites close to the river or main roads. As a result of land dealing, asset-stripping and speculation, land values rose from about £150,000 per acre for office land in 1968 to over £1 million in 1972. This had an immediate effect on rents and encouraged landlords to terminate leases as soon as they fell due. Dereliction spread rapidly as industries closed down and land-owners held out for permission to redevelop.

The second process is through the 'externality' effects of new developments. New projects such as offices encouraged associated uses such as sandwich bars and camera shops. Often these uses came as part of a complete development package and were regarded by the planners as planning gain 'for the community'. Uses that the community might have regarded as more beneficial such as family housing, neighbourhood shops, play space, or light industry were not considered compatible with office developments for social reasons (not a good area to bring up families) and at the same time were ruled out on economic grounds being 'low value' land uses. This thinking by the planners and developers was a recognition that a good quality office development does not come on its own but must come with related car parks, executive flats, restaurants, and a pleasant environment for office workers. Indeed, at the present time, estate agents note that one of the problems with North Southwark is the shortage of shops for office workers due to the fact that the large development packages have not yet been completed. But when these are finished, a new working environment will be available which should sustain the growth of offices still further.

The third way in which redevelopment affects the area is through a characteristic pattern of chain reactions where one development is used by the planners to justify another. Thus a planning application to redevelop a row of neighbourhood shops was used to justify the redevelopment of other shops in the area which it was said would be located in the new centre. Another example, was the designation of an area as 'soft' from a redevelopment point of view because planning permissions for offices in the area had already been granted. Another example of a different kind of chain, was a case where the Council negotiated a new library as planning gain (even though there was already a library in the area) but found itself having to foot the bill when the developers (Fairfields) refused to pay the increased cost of the new library. This dilemma forced the Council to consider selling the old library site to subsidize the 'planning gain'.

These three processes illustrate the almost overwhelming lack of control of redevelopment by the Southwark planners and the consequent lack of any real planning as far as the local community was concerned. The real planning process in this situation was the economic logic of the property market with the planners granting formal approval at each stage.

But what was the human impact of this economic logic? Of foremost importance was the loss of industrial jobs. Industry had been in slow decline in Southwark years before Hays Wharf closed, but the closure of Hays and the publication of the Strategy Plan triggered off a sharp fall. Between 1967–72, over 17,000 industrial jobs were lost. Each of the traditional industries, transport, engineering, printing, food and drink, and docking suffered heavy losses as plants closed down or moved out. Not all of these jobs meant redundancies because some workers moved with the firms but Department of Employment statistics show that there were over 8,000 official redundancies in that period and according to the 1971 Census Southwark had a higher unemployment rate than any other London Borough.

The run down of industry is still taking place. A census of industry undertaken by the North Southwark Community Development Group, in 1974, covering the fifty largest firms showed that out of 6,085 jobs, 1,657 or 27% were likely to be lost through closures within the next two or three years. This represents a loss of fifteen firms, more than half of which are in the printing industry. Added to this, even in firms where the management are adamant that the firm will not move, rumours of closure are rife among the workers and there is considerable fear of redundancy, a fear that is obviously aggravated during a general recession.

The human cost is not easy to assess objectively. Planners have argued that people laid off work in London have usually a good chance of getting another job. Others have said that redundancy payments compensate for the loss of a job. But the careful study of redundancy in south-east London by Daniel in 1972 showed that these assumptions are highly misleading. Daniel found that many of the workers he surveyed (all from engineering firms) who looked for other work suffered a loss of real earnings after they had found another job. Losses increased with age, amounting to 13% for those between forty-six and fifty-five years of age to 29% for those between fifty-six and sixty-five years of age. Moreover, the increase in journey to work times was on average 18%, but rose with age to nearly 40% for workers over forty-six. Studies of firms closing in Southwark have revealed a similar pattern.

In North Southwark, unskilled workers, particularly if they are married women, do not usually stay with a firm which moves outside inner south-east London. The further away the firm moves the more workers leave or are laid off. Some skilled workers may be prepared to travel quite long distances to keep their jobs, but others will not, especially if the firm is relocating outside London.

When a firm closes the main task for the union is to negotiate the largest possible redundancy payment and to find alternative work for its members. Many unions representing skilled trades such as printing, docking and transport already have long waiting lists in the London area so that the effects of redevelopment pose an additional problem for them. Redundancy payments, though depending upon how long a worker has been with the firm, usually amount to the equivalent of a few months' employment so that they cannot be considered any answer to the problem of industrial decline.

The planners often contend that though there may be a temporary problem caused by the closure of industrial firms in Central London, in the long term the problem will be solved by the 'preference' of young people for office jobs, that is the type of job that is to be provided by means of the Strategy Plan; the right 'job mix', as it is called, is on the way. However, this view rests on the assumptions that all young people seek and are qualified for office work and that all older workers should be written off. It is difficult to understand how a Labour controlled Council could accept these assumptions.

A further assumption that must be considered is that Southwark residents will have access to office jobs coming into the Borough in areas like North Southwark. But the system of Office Development Permits virtually ensures that an office moving into North Southwark is moving lock, stock, and barrel from somewhere else in London and as often as not this is the City. Thus, the firm is likely to bring its entire labour force with it. This is the case with all of the large office blocks planned for Thameside. The gain in jobs for Southwark residents will be very small. For example, the office block to be developed by Laings is to be occupied by the Alex Howden insurance group who reckon that all but about thirty jobs will come straight across the river from their premises in the City. On top of this, there is no shortage of secretarial, cleaning, and general service jobs in Central London so that the existence of several hundreds or thousands more of these jobs in North Southwark is not likely to be a great benefit to the residents.

Finally, is must be said that one of the present advantages of manual industrial work is that it is on the whole well paid and that alternative office or service work pays inferior wages for more hours works. Thus, the loss of an industrial job in London leads to a reduction in the real earnings of Londoners. And as the cost of living in London continues to rise, this is a very important consideration.

We have regarded jobs as one of the major problems created by redevelopment in North Southwark but what are the other problems? The community itself is probably most affected by the closure of the local shops and community facilities. Throughout Inner London the number of neighbourhood shops is on the decline, but the rate of decline is most severe where redevelopment is taking place and where rents are going up. North Southwark has both of these problems. Redevelopment of local shopping parades for office and shop complexes is very common throughout the area. The new shops are inevitably expensive and of a different character unless the local authority subsidizes shopkeepers through low rents. The general pattern of shopping changes from a scatter of small shops to the concentration of shops in selected parades and in large regional centres such as the Elephant and Castle. This suits the planners, developers, and shopkeepers but it is doubtful if local residents, especially the elderly, who find it difficult to get about, are satisfied.

The closure of chemist shops in North Southwark illustrates the issues well. From 1973–4, five dispensing chemists in North Southwark closed as a result of redevelopment, high rents, and Boots' policy to close all low-profit chemist shops. Chemists make their money not out of prescriptions but out of the sales of non-dispensing goods such as cosmetics and toothpaste and the sales of these items must be very large to cover the high cost (about £4,000 a year) of paying a pharmacist. But in an area of slowly declining population, sales of non-dispensing goods are dropping in many cases, while at the same time other costs such as rents are going up. Thus, whatever the demand for prescriptions in the area, and in North Southwark nearly 20% of the population are pensioners, only a few chemists can survive, with the result that residents must walk further to their nearest chemist, therefore adding to the hardship of living in the area.

Redevelopment has also brought an atmosphere of isolation and dereliction. We have already said that many industrial premises are empty, but also shops are boarded up, and there is a general air of uncertainty. Some housing estates are now isolated as slum clearance and industrial closure has taken place, while office buildings have created a deadening effect on the area at nights and on weekends. The overall physical environment is not a pleasant one for most people and it is not, therefore, surprising that many residents would move out if they had the chance.

No residents would argue that they were satisfied with the area before redevelopment began but few believe that it has improved things or that, when it is over, the community will be better off. What the community sees is the concentration of attention by the planning system on the commercial and industrial buildings in the area rather than on the existing community. Re-zoning commercial and industrial buildings for central area uses makes no positive contribution to the large residential population which will remain long after the developers have moved on elsewhere.

Adding up the Costs and Benefits

One of the reasons for taking such a detailed look at the impact of the redevelopment process on North Southwark is to draw some fairly objective conclusions about the costs and benefits of the process. We have implied already that redevelopment has been responsible for the loss of jobs, community facilities, and the erosion of the community but it is impossible to say how many of the changes in the area have been due to redevelopment on its own compared with other economic forces. All we can say is that redevelopment was a powerful contributory factor in these changes and that is has contributed to some clear costs and benefits. These we have assembled under four headings.

1. *The Local Area.* Out of a total of 77,000 jobs of all kinds in

1967, 17,000 industrial jobs were lost between 1967–72. Recent surveys indicate that a further 10,000 jobs could be lost between 1972–6. These jobs were held by workers from all over south-east London and, though there are other industrial manual jobs in south-east London, the dramatic decline of North Southwark as an industrial area has reduced the choice of skilled manual jobs in inner London and has increased the distance that workers have to travel to these types of jobs. Thus, throughout south-east London, including North Southwark, residents are having to commute further and further to work. Though acknowledging these social costs, the Southwark Council argues that they will be partly offset by the creation of over 20,000 office jobs in the borough. The present evidence, however, is that most of these jobs will not be new jobs for local people and anyhow will be held by commuters from outer London.

Local residents, though concerned with the changing job structure of the area, are more concerned at the moment with the loss of amenities and the general deterioration of the environment caused by redevelopment pressures. Southwark Council has insisted that these difficulties are only temporary and that facilities such as shops and theatres built for office workers and tourists will benefit residents too. But residents see no indications that inconvenience will be only temporary and find that most new facilities are not geared to their needs and that the local cost of living is rising above that of most other working-class areas.

2. *Other Areas.* To some extent the problems of North Southwark have benefited other areas of the country, including other areas of London. For example, some of the firms which have moved out have gone to the new towns, or to regions, or to outer London. Similarly, Southwark Council has argued on many occasions that new theatres, hotels, and riverside walks will benefit 'all of London'. No doubt these benefits do exist but the question with which we are concerned is *which* Londoners are likely to benefit most. Many suspect that when the Council talks about London as a whole they are thinking more of Chelsea or the City of London rather than Bermondsey or the East End. On other occasions there seems to be a greater concern for tourists than for the thousands on the Council waiting list.

3. *The Local Authority*. The Borough of Southwark as a corporate body foresees many benefits from the redevelopment of the northern part of the Borough. Faced with a huge capital debt, rising costs, and government cut-backs, the Council is anxious to boost rateable values wherever it can. Indeed some councillors have stated that housing and social services programmes will have to be cut back unless developments producing large rate revenues can be attracted to the Borough. Thus, the Council, in competition with other inner London boroughs, is actively seeking large development schemes irrespective of their social or planning merit. But in practice only about a quarter of these new revenues will be available to Southwark. The rest will be divided between the GLC, Inner London Education Authority, the Metropolitan Police and the Thames Water Authority giving these authorities their own stake in the promotion of profitable development projects. These authorities tend to forget that such developments create new social and economic problems which must be met with added social service and housing expenditure.

In addition to rate revenue, the Southwark Council has argued that redevelopment will provide benefits to the Borough and to the community in the form of planning gains. But quite apart from the fact that these planning gains are often little more than bribes to obtain planning permission, they often seem much more likely to benefit tourists and better-off Londoners than the local community or those on the housing list. For example, the planning gains from the massive Edgers Investments office block (557,000 sq. ft) are on close examination of little local benefit. The developers offered to build a riverside walk, to make a contribution to landscaping the scheme, and to give two acres of land for open space, and about an acre of land on which the Council could build flats. Who will these planning gains be for? The riverside walk is a tourist feature (there has always been a road running beside the river at that point), the landscaping seems more likely to enhance the office block, the open space is an awkward triangular shape and will be unsuitable for football or general running around, and finally the flats will be single-person flats and therefore will not alleviate the shortage of family housing in the area or in Southwark as a whole. Consequently, these planning gains do not help Southwark Council solve its problems or the problems of the area but are simply ways of justifying the granting of a hugely profitable planning permission.

An even more serious charge against the Council's redevelopment strategy is that with an acute housing crisis in Inner London and a waiting list of its own of over 9,300, Southwark is giving away land on which council housing ought to be built. But the Council have staunchly held the view that not only does it have the best housing record of all the London boroughs but that it has more than enough land to fulfil its housing obligations. It claims that 2,000 dwellings will be built on the Surrey Docks and that this will solve many of the Borough's housing problems. In addition, the Council argues that places like the Surrey Docks are much more suitable areas for family housing than the Thames-side because a proper 'social infrastructure' can be created on Surrey Docks but not on Thames-side. Such arguments are, however, of little comfort for those on the waiting list or for those already living in North Southwark who are pressing for the community to be consolidated after many years of decline.

The case for building up the community is an important one. Population decline and redevelopment have combined to fragment the community and erode its facilities. The proportion of pensioners is increasing and young people must move outside the area to find accommodation. There is thus no benefit to the community from increased office development nor from supplying token amounts of single-person accommodation as a planning gain.

4. *The Development Industry.* In simple wealth-distribution terms, the outstanding beneficiaries of the redevelopment of North Southwark are the various groups that make up the development industry. When the Strategy Plan came out, various estimates were made of how much wealth would be extracted from land sales and redevelopment. Under the assumption of a net increase in office space of 4 million sq. ft and applying property values prevailing at the height of the boom, estimates of gross profit ranged from £800 million to £2,000 million. But since only a few redevelopments were completed before the property boom ended, these estimates must now be revised. A further new factor to be considered is the recent change (1975)

in the GLC policy towards offices in central London which is almost certainly going to restrict the increase in office space in North Southwark. All that we can do, therefore, is to indicate the approximate distribution of benefits among different sections of the population.

We can begin with the profits made before redevelopment began. Plots of land were sold at inflated prices throughout the Strategy Plan area especially in the areas zoned for West End uses in the GLDP and the Strategy Plan. At a conservative estimate deals worth between £70 million and £100 million were made, almost all of which was profit since no development gains tax was due at that time. These profits went to historic landowners and to property and investment companies. There was also widespread speculation in the shares of the principal property groups in North Southwark sometimes as a direct result of press comment on the progress of redevelopment plans. Shareholders in Hays Wharf, Amalgamated Investment and Property, Edgers Investments, and Sterling Guarantee particularly benefited from this speculation.

What sort of wealth distribution is associated with speculation in these property shares? Some indication can be obtained from the ownership of the shares of some of the prominent property companies operating in North Southwark. For example, in 1973 there were 75 million ordinary shares of the Amalgamated Investment and Property Company of which 7% were held by the directors. The chairman alone held 3½ million shares, worth £2.6 million at the time, and producing £52,500 before tax on the dividends. The St Martin's Property Corporation, another company with a large stake in the Hays Wharf development, had in 1973, 6,350 shareholders owning a total of 60 million ordinary shares. The directors between them held four million shares worth £60,560 in dividends. In both of these companies, financial institutions own some of the shares but we do not know what the proportions are.

The distribution of shares in smaller property companies active in North Southwark is even more restricted. For example, the Fairfield Property Company which is particularly evident in Borough High Street has only four shareholders all of whom are directors of the company. Another small company, Crowne

Freeholds, is effectively controlled by one family. Therefore, although larger companies have a slightly wider spread of share ownership than small firms, the profits from the redevelopment of North Southwark have gone to a tiny group of people, many of whom already held either land in North Southwark or a stake in the property industry. By no stretch of the imagination was there a significant expansion in the ownership of property profits as a result of the property boom in North Southwark.

Conclusions

North Southwark was in the front line of redevelopment in London during the property boom principally because of its location next to the City of London but also because the planning authorities decided to change the zoning of large areas to 'West End Uses'. From the subsequent invasion of office development and blight, the property industry has been the clear beneficiary with the local community the outright loser. Somewhere in the middle, the Labour controlled Southwark Council has attempted to justify its almost complete lack of control over the redevelopment process with promises of long-term rate revenues and dubious planning gains. Throughout the entire episode, the Council has not only accepted without protest the difficult planning situation in which they found themselves but has even welcomed the opportunities to create a cleaner, shinier North Southwark.

One of the most striking aspects of the whole process is the capacity of the planners and Labour councillors to come up with the most astonishing rationalizations for their actions. For example, they have argued that full consultation with the community is not necessary 'at this stage' because the Thames-side Plan is 'only' a Strategy Plan and that proper consultation will come with the eventual preparation of Local Plans. They have argued that the riverside is 'not suitable for family housing' and that in planning terms the local area could be better served by building mixed development interspersed here and there with single-person accommodation which is said to be more compatible with 'mixed uses'. Finally, they have said that since North Southwark is so close to Central London (i.e. the City and West End), it should be developed for land uses which are 'more appropriate' to this location. These are of course precisely the arguments used by the developers and their advisers to justify their own schemes.

Chapter 5 The Property Development
System in Brighton

At their meeting on Thursday, 13 December 1973, the former
Brighton Borough Council voted on party lines to accept the
recommendation of their Planning Committee that outline planning permission should be given to British Rail and Peachey
Property Corporation, to redevelop their twenty-five-acre Brighton Station site. The permission (which was dependent on minor
modifications being made) was for a new station, a large hotel,
conference facilities, a hypermarket, a vast car park, a telecommunications centre, a recreation centre, a small amount of housing and 250,000 sq. ft of 'general offices with parking'. This was
by no means the end of the story as this chapter will show. But
had the council been the sole arbiters the consent would have
been given and this development would have gone ahead. Earlier
in the year, the Labour group on the Council had seen their
alternative proposals voted down. Their scheme had been to
preserve and restore the Victorian station and to build 760 units
of council housing on the half of the site not currently used by
the station. This could have had the effect of housing over one
half of those on the Council's waiting list.

Tory councillors used a variety of arguments to support the
British Rail proposals. Some stressed the need for more parking
for the convenience of conference visitors, some dwelt on the
problems faced by those getting out of the back four coaches of
a twelve-coach train on a wet day; the existing station canopy
is not quite long enough to keep them dry. One, somewhat more
relevantly, pointed out that the site was worth millions and could
not possibly be used for council housing. It was also stated more
than once that the Labour group were against progress for the
town. The Conservatives insisted that they still supported the
agreed policy of restraining the use of the car in the *centre* of the
town, but they argued that as this particular site was on the

fringe of the town, the traffic it would undoubedly generate would not add to Brighton's problems (although in the Brighton *Evening Argus* of 19 June 1973, a Conservative councillor referred to the site as '. . . this . . . very important central site'). In any case, 'if we were to restrain the motor car we would be sounding the deathknell of the town.'

This chapter will examine these events more closely and will focus upon the underlying capitalist logic that dictates them. The issue is whether a 'windfall' site in a town short of land should be used for commercial purposes or to accommodate a large addition to the town's stock of low-cost housing. The parties to the conflict can be easily identified. On the one hand a big public corporation and a commercial developer who between them stand to make millions, a bevy of highly paid consultants and professional advisers, and the general business interests in the town. On the other the 'Save Brighton Station' campaign (a widely based pressure group), the Labour group on the Council, several local 'alternative' newspapers and, most important, the thousands of families on the waiting-list and the 17,000 inadequately housed in the town. A brief review of the planning context and local housing conditions will provide a basis for deciding which outcome would best serve the most pressing needs in the town.

The town of Brighton forms part of an urbanized strip stretching along the Sussex coast from Seaford to Littlehampton. This strip is hemmed in on the north by tracts of chalk downland, nearly all of which is strictly protected from development. London is fifty miles to the north, up a main railway line which runs through three other areas of rapid employment growth: Haywards Heath/Burgess Hill, Crawley and Croydon. Because of the severe problems of land shortage and of the pre-1974 fragmentation of the urban entity between three planning authorities, Brighton, East Sussex and West Sussex, the area was among the first in the country to be asked to prepare a structure plan under the 1968 Town and Country Planning Act. The *Greater Brighton Structure Plan*, which is an extremely useful source of information, was eventually produced.

It was, however, superseded on 1 April 1974, when Brighton became a district of the new East Sussex County Council and thus lost its strategic planning powers to the county. The county was itself engaged on the preparation of a countywide structure plan which, at the time of writing, has just been presented in the form of a hastily prepared consultative draft. This document is such that almost *any* development pattern could emerge and still be consistent with it. Both structure plans were prepared in the general planning context provided by the *Strategic Plan for the South East* which was published in 1970. This plan, which is non-statutory and therefore in no way legally binding, deals with the whole of the south-east region and specifies to planning authorities the overall pattern of growth to be worked towards from now till the end of the century. One of the aims of this chapter is to assess the extent to which developments in Brighton are consistent with the framework provided by the regional plan (which proposed very limited growth for the area) and by the two structure plans.

The 1971 Census showed that Brighton and Hove together had a combined population of about 234,000 in 1971, 106,000 male and 128,000 female. This represents a slight decrease compared to 1961 (236,000). The sex imbalance is due largely to a higher than national proportion of people over retirement age (nearly 27%) and there is in particular a very large number of widows. Given the level of pensions, and the effects of rapid inflation on fixed incomes, this means a large pool of people with slender resources. Because of the age structure and the sex imbalance, the area has a built-in tendency to natural population decrease which was almost balanced in the period 1961–71 by net immigration. But shortage of land, and thus housing, is a constraint on population inflow. The high incidence of low-paid and seasonally fluctuating service employment conspires to produce an 'at risk' population rather larger than might otherwise be expected. The dependent population (children under fourteen and people over retirement age) number 742 for 1,000 of working population. This is some way above the national average and it underlines the need for sensitive and comprehensive housing and health provision policies.

The Local Housing Situation

Although the population level of the area is roughly constant, the housing situation seems to be moving from a state of stress to a state of crisis. According to the 1971 Census there was a total of 92,440 dwellings in Brighton and Hove, distributed as follows

Owner occupied	44%
Local authority	17
Privately rented (unfurnished)	28
Privately rented (furnished)	11
	100%

The area thus has an under-representation of owner-occupiers (nationally 52%) and of local authority tenants (nationally 28%). By contrast, 28% of dwellings in Brighton and 49% of those in Hove are flats (compared to the national proportion of 10%). The very large privately rented sector incorporates most of the area's housing problems since well over half the flats are in converted buildings and about half of the total stock was built before 1908. Conditions in this large privately rented sector leave much to be desired. Whereas over 90% of both owner-occupiers and council tenants have the exclusive use of the three basic amenities – hot water, a bath or shower and an inside flush toilet – the corresponding percentage in the unfurnished rented sector is 62% and in the furnished sector 37%. In addition to all this, 3,526 households in Brighton and Hove in 1971 were overcrowded by current planning standards.

All indications for the future are that the situation is likely to get rapidly worse. A fall in household size is expected so that even if population remains constant more dwellings will be needed. In November 1973, the Chief Officers (the Town Clerk, the Borough Treasurer, Architect, Planning Officer, Housing Officer and so on) reported to the Council that the average income necessary to get a council mortgage to purchase a £12,000 house was £77 per week. This compares with the 1972 regional male average wage of £33.80. At the same time there has been a drop in the supply of rented accommodation in Brighton from about 21,000 units in 1961 to 20,290 in 1971, mainly because landlords have powerful financial incentives to obtain vacant possession and sell their properties, and the rate at which the supply is drying up has probably accelerated since 1971. In addition, the 1974 Rent Act, which extended security of tenure to furnished lettings, has probably acted to some extent as a disincentive to landlords in this sector. The 'unavailable dwellings', which include empty houses and second homes, are currently 7% of total stock in Brighton and the proportion is expected to rise to 9% or 10%.

It has been estimated that the student population of the area is likely to rise from the 1974 figure of 8,000 to about 14,000 in 1981. Of this 1974 figure very nearly 5,000 were competing with local residents for housing space. Even given the most optimistic assumptions about new accommodation on the various campuses, this figure seems certain to rise to over 6,300 by 1981 and all this increase will fall upon the privately rented sector. Since students can get together in groups of five or more and each contribute, say, £5 towards the rent, it is evident that they can easily outbid the average family for, say, a four-roomed flat. If the proportion of students housed on campus remains at its present level (20%) rather than rising to 40% as proposed, then the impact on the area by 1981 is not an extra 1,300 students but an extra 4,200. This would pose an extremely severe extra burden on a desperately stretched system.

Overall, therefore, the outlook is grave and its gravity has been recognized by Labour and Conservative councillors alike:

Brighton is becoming a ghetto for the old and the rich.
(Councillor Hobden, Labour, 18 May 1973)

. . . Something must be done to stop our young people from leaving this town because they cannot buy or rent property within their price range, unless we are prepared to sit back and watch Brighton become a town of old folk like some other towns on the south coast.
(Councillor Mrs Vale, Conservative, letter to Brighton Housing Committee, February 1973)

Similar sentiments have been voiced by the local paper:

A major rethink of the whole housing problem . . . is necessary if a new class of deprived person is to be avoided.
(*Evening Argus*, Opinion, 2 June 1972)

Despite these statements, the number of local authority houses completed in Brighton and Hove combined has fallen from about 300 units in 1970 to an average of about 200 units in 1974–5 while the total of those waiting for council housing has risen from 1,586 to 2,381 at the end of 1974. Clearly some acceleration in local house building programmes is necessary. Brighton's Chief Officers, in their report to the Council in late 1973, drew attention to some of the problems and set out building requirements for 1986 and 2001. At the subsequent Council meeting, it was agreed, despite Labour opposition, that the combined local authority and housing association component in the town's total stock should not be allowed to rise above a target figure of 25%. No argument was advanced to support this decision except that the percentage was well above that of Bournemouth; 'a town with which we often compare notes'.

To get to this 25% target, an extra 3,450 council or housing association houses will be needed in view of expected population growth between 1971 and 1986. Since only 813 were added to the stock between 1961 and 1971 (an increase of 7%), the building rate will have to be stepped up. A number of earmarked sites were listed in the officers' report, but to reach the necessary target 900 houses would have to be built in areas of outstanding natural beauty, two hospitals would have to be knocked down and built elsewhere and space for 650 houses would need to be found in central sites. The chance of all this happening by 1986 seems fairly remote. The conclusions from these figures seem clear. Given the problems associated with the private sector, both owned and rented, every effort must be made by the authority to find land, and sites that become available (such as the station site) should be used to produce low-cost housing. The alternative will be a further worsening of present conditions.

Trends in Office Development

In marked contrast to the poor house building record, office development in the local area has gone ahead strongly in recent years. Rent levels for newly built space in central Brighton have risen from about 50–60p per sq. ft in 1961 to £3 or more in 1974–5. As we have seen, this is the basis for the greater profitability of developing offices rather than factories or housing. One reason for the strong rental growth has been the popularity of Brighton and Hove as alternatives to London and Croydon for employers unable to find space in the larger centres.

A number of analyses of this situation have recently been made. The *Greater Brighton Structure Plan* pointed out that between 1964 and 1970 office space in Brighton and Hove increased by about 44%. As we have seen, the amount of council housing increased by only 7% over a rather longer period (1961–71). The Structure Plan team were naturally concerned at this imbalance. They pointed out that this was a more rapid office growth rate than the south-east as a whole had experienced; they reiterated warnings about the physical constraints imposed by the Downs; they drew attention to the possible conflict between the needs of commerce and the social preferences of the community; and they pointed out the obvious labour shortages that would result from a serious mismatch between the growth of offices and housing. They concluded (in 1971) that the 'continuance of past rates of building could lead to an excess demand for office workers and the need for a radical reappraisal of office development policy'.

Concurrently with the structure team's study, the Brighton Planning Officer was preparing a report (dated 24 February 1972) on Office Employment in Brighton for members of the town's Corporate Estates and Planning Committees. This '. . . attempts to explain in simple language the problems of an expansion of office development in Brighton . . .' The report drew attention to an increase in the amount of unoccupied office space from 1966 to 1971 (from 'very little' to approximately 150,000 sq. ft). The Planning Officer pointed out that if all the office developments listed for 1976 were carried out there could be a shortage of some 10,000 office workers and the deficiency would increase towards the end of the decade. He concluded that the extension of the restrictions on the granting of office development permits until 1977 would help (the government have subsequently done this) and pointed out the regional implications of a large-scale office building programme:

. . . firstly, there would be a greater demand for housing for which there is already a shortage of land in Brighton, and secondly, there would be an increase in the journey to work traffic from those living outside the area who could not find housing within the area.

He recommended that

To maintain a balance between land uses in the town centre any appreciable increase in offices should be matched by an appropriate amount of residential use.
(The reference to the town centre should be noted.)

A further report from the Chief Officers was presented to the June, 1974 meeting of the new Brighton Council's Policy and Resources Committee. This indicated that an annual increase of 33,900 sq. ft of commercial office floorspace would be consistent with the long-term intentions of the *Greater Brighton Structure Plan* and the 1970 *Strategic Plan for the South East*. However, the annual report pointed out that between 1965 and 1972 new office space had been added at nearly twice this annual rate. Furthermore, as at 31 March 1974, consents for a further 795,590 sq. ft had already been granted. This represented nearly twenty-five years' worth of development at the recommended rate. It was calculated that this amount of new office floorspace would generate, ignoring all other factors, a demand for 2,600 new dwellings, thus causing 'extremely serious pressures for growth in an area which is seriously short of residential land'. The report concluded that, in general terms, no further permissions should be given for commercial office space except that 'where exceptional circumstances exist they should be treated on their merits'. Just four months after the report was adopted, two 'exceptional' cases had already been given consents.

The situation is, in essence, quite simple. Report after report has warned of the dangers of an imbalance between the rate of growth of offices and of housing and other support services. Inevitably, if workers are to fill the new offices, more commuting from outside the town will be necessary. In fact at a meeting of the adjacent East Sussex County Council on 15 May 1973 it was pointed out that a survey had shown that three quarters of office workers in the Preston Park area of Brighton actually lived in Haywards Heath or Burgess Hill. This situation naturally cannot help these neighbouring authorities to achieve a balanced employment/population growth policy and to avoid a labour shortage. As the chairman of the county's Planning Committee pointed out; 'Brighton is hoping to build more offices, but it does nothing to provide the social services, education or housing for the office workers it attracts'. But unfortunately, 'This authority cannot give an instruction to Brighton'.

The effects of the office consents outstanding at March 1974, was to provide for a further 795,000 sq. ft of office space. If the proposals for the Station and Jubilee Street, which will be discussed subsequently, are passed then approximately 425,000 sq. ft of *additional* commercial office floorspace would be added bringing Brighton's total to something over 2.7 million sq. ft by the end of the 1970s; getting on for three times the figure in 1965. Growth on this scale, in the absence of a massive housing programme, must mean a host of problems not only for Brighton and Hove but also for the sub-region as a whole. The lengthening housing waiting lists, already mentioned, are just one of these problems. It is in this general planning context that we approach the two case studies; Brighton Station and the Jubilee Street redevelopment.

The Planning / Development System at Work

Brighton Station

We can now return to the planning issue with which the chapter began; the proposed redevelopment of the twenty-five-acre Brighton Station site owned by British Rail. At present the station itself occupies about half of the site, two acres are used by National Carriers and most of the rest is used for car parking. The land is zoned for 'railway use' in the 1958 *Development Plan*. Since no subsequent structure plan has yet been approved, the 1958 plan is still the statutory context for planning in the town. The station is of some architectural distinction, having been built by David Mocatta in 1841, and its loss would be a matter for national concern.

Following at least four years' work behind the scenes, British Rail and the Peachey Property Corporation made public their proposals for the site in April 1973, on the day before Good Friday; the Planning Committee was to meet the following Tuesday. They applied in outline for a re-zoning of the land and for the replacement of the existing station with a 'glamorous' new one. Other land uses proposed in the application included:

– a hotel (550 rooms) and service flats
– a conference centre
– 5.4 acres of residential flats 'in a wide price range' (of which 3.3 acres would go to local authority or housing association use)
– public car parking (1,000 car spaces)
– a Post Office Telecommunications Centre
– an all-weather recreation centre
– general offices and parking

A British Rail Property Board spokesman acknowledged that the Board was aware of the merits of Victorian architecture but pointed out that they had an obligation to develop railway land in a way which would best benefit railway finances. People with a wide range of interests immediately opposed the proposals. A group of Labour councillors cabled the chairman of British Rail urging the withdrawal of the application and within a few days another group wrote to the Department of the Environment asking for the station to be put on the list of buildings of special architectural or historic interest. The Department complied with surprising speed. Protests began to flood in and the 'Save Brighton Station' campaign alone delivered 963 protests during the three weeks subsequent to the publication of the plan.

The Labour group on Brighton Borough Council began to take up some of the 'Save Brighton Station' arguments and to articulate them in the Council. These were that large-scale office developments here would not be consistent with the regionally based limited growth policy for the coastal strip, and therefore Office Development Permits might not be granted. (No Office Development Permit was attached with the planning application; a point which became crucially significant later.) Neither were British Rail's intentions consistent with central government policies that surplus railway land should be offered to local authorities to meet local needs. Offices and car parking on the scale proposed would imply road developments (including a north–south 'spine' road) not dissimilar to those proposed by the consultants Wilson and Womersley in a recently prepared report on traffic management in central Brighton; a report which the Council had decisively rejected only months earlier in view of the housing loss that its roadbuilding proposals would imply.

In addition, the British Rail proposals would do very little to relieve the increasingly desperate housing situation and there could be no guarantee that the 3.3 acres of intended low-income housing would actually end up that way. Finally, it was argued, the station was an important piece of architecture and could easily be refurbished. The 'Save Brighton Station' group urged the Department of the Environment to ensure that the widest possible public debate should occur, if necessary in the form of a public inquiry, in view of the importance of the site to Brighton. They also pointed out that it would be a 'cynical repudiation, of the whole structure plan concept if the approval were given before a local plan had been drawn up for the area'. (It will be evident from earlier sections of this chapter, that any further office approvals would be totally inconsistent with strategic planning intentions.)

Taking all these considerations into account, the Labour group, mindful of the worsening housing situation in the town, worked out an alternative scheme. This was to leave the station as it was, to obtain a Compulsory Purchase Order for the rest of the site and to develop the land thus acquired for local authority housing. The group submitted their own planning application for 760 low-rise housing units which would have had the effect of clearing a large proportion of the Council's waiting list. It would have been entirely consistent with all the advice the Council had been receiving concerning the balanced growth of offices and housing in the town, and especially in its central areas. It would have been consistent, too, with the government's view, expressed in the white paper 'Widening the Choice' that surplus nationalized industry land should be released for housing purposes.

The Planning Committee deferred this application and asked the Council's Chief Officers for their views of the alternative proposals. The officers reported back to the Planning Committee and the Finance Committee, but not, curiously, to the Housing Committee whose problems the Labour proposals were primarily aimed to solve. In a fairly evenly balanced report they suggested that:

. . . an alternative to compulsory acquisition, which may secure the desired objective, would be to discuss with British Rail the inclusion within their proposals of other developments and uses preferred by the local authority.

But they also pointed out that compulsory purchase would give the Council positive power over the site rather than '. . . the negative powers conferred by normal development control'.

On the key issue of the value of the land, and thus the cost of compulsory purchase to the local authority, they pointed out that the value of any site hinges upon the use to which it may be put. The arbitration procedure necessary to arrive at a compulsory purchase value would need to take account of the fact that an application for office and other commercial development had been put forward which, if granted, would confer greater value on the site than its current use value. Despite these uncertainties, the officers estimated a value of £3 million. Using this figure, they calculated the annual cost of a possible council housing development. Assuming that 720 flats (for 2,000 people) were placed on the site (a development similar to that proposed by the Labour group), the total capital cost, including land, would be about £7.3 million. The annual financing cost would be £527,000. Assuming 'fair rents' of £7 per week, and the usual government subsidy of 75% of the annual cost, the total burden to the rates would be a mere £132,000 per year. The officers concluded:

It will be seen that the proposition to purchase compulsorily and to develop is perfectly feasible provided the greatest obstacle in its way [i.e. the confirmation by the Secretary of State] can be overcome.

The officers' advice made the Labour group's proposals look very practical. However, housebuilding on this scale would reduce local housing scarcity and might possibly lead to falling house values and rents. For the property lobby this would be a most unwelcome outcome. Rather than pursuing the compulsory purchase idea it was decided that renegotiations should take place with British Rail/Peachey Property Corporation with a view to securing better 'planning gain' for the town and especially to secure the release of some land 'to meet Brighton's essential needs'. The chairmen of three committees, finance, planning, and highways and transport, were to be the prime negotiators. (The omission of the Housing Committee's chairman is curious, and perhaps indicative of the Council's priorities). The idea of a CPO was to be given no further consideration unless these negotiations proved abortive, and it was, in fact, finally voted out on 28 June 1973 thus nullifying the Labour group's planning application.

The outcome of the renegotiation was a further planning application from British Rail which included the following proposed uses (in the approximate order in which they would be built):

– a new station
– a hotel (1,000 beds)
– a conference centre (1,500 capacity)
– a hypermarket (100,000 sq. ft) plus 900 car spaces
– service flats plus 100 flats for sale or lease plus parking
– offices (250,000 sq. ft) plus parking
– an office and depot for Seeboard
– a public car park (2,000 car spaces)
– 150 flats for local authority/housing association use
– GPO offices and telephone exchange
– an all-season recration centre

These proposals for a highly congested town centre site have, in all the circumstances, a majestic sweep and originality. The effect of the renegotiation, undertaken it will be remembered to increase the 'essential to the town' component, was to double the size of the hotel, to more than double the parking space, not to increase the housing provision, to specify the office component and, most original of all, to produce a hypermarket. Hypermarkets are extremely large, all-purpose shops designed primarily for the car-borne shopper. Even in north America, the land of their birth, they usually get themselves located on urban fringes or in open country. To propose one for a highly congested central site, in the same year that a policy of town centre 'traffic restraint' had found support on all sides, was a genuine *coup*.

The Labour group submitted written and oral objections on grounds which it would by now be wearisome to repeat. The

Chief Officers, in conjunction with the Director of Resort and Conference Services and, finally, the Housing Manager, again submitted their views to Planning Committee. But the tone of their report was now (November 1973) markedly pro-development:

. . . its (the station's) exterior does no credit whatsoever to its surroundings . . . We believe that the advantages to the town of the proposed development greatly outweigh the desirability of retaining this old building.

The class of hotel proposed by the developers is one which nowadays demands that there shall always be associated conference facilities . . .

We can see no objection to the proposal to provide 250,000 sq. ft of office accommodation . . .

(Although most, if not all, the signatories must have known that office development on this scale would be totally inconsistent with all long-term planning intentions.)

In relation to the estimated 4,500 parking spaces on the site:

There is no disputing that considerable traffic movements will be generated by the development . . . however . . . unless this area is to remain sterile, any development of it will generate substantial movement.

(It is, of course, well known that some land uses generate much more traffic movement than others.)

To summarize, the basic issues before the Committee are the changes in zoning of the Development Plan and the loss of the station . . .

Certainly these issues were the immediate ones but in the total context of the situation, the basic issue was whether the site should be used for offices and shops or for housing – for private profit or for public benefit. Finally:

Most of the land uses proposed are such as to be expected in town centre redevelopment.

This is the crux of the matter. Under a capitalist property system, central land is potentially very profitable.

At its meeting on 13 December 1973 the Council decided that it was minded to grant outline permission for the scheme. Some of the arguments used in favour were set out at the beginning of the chapter. Apart from these, one Conservative councillor declared that the rate revenue generated by the scheme could be used to improve the social services which were '. . . so much at the heart of our thinking'. He also felt it would solve the town's unemployment problem, thus failing to distinguish between the needs of unemployed low-skill manual workers and the massive labour shortage in the office sector which occurs virtually all over the region.

Events from this point on should be seen in the context of the changes which local government reorganization were to bring about on 1 April 1974. At this date Brighton was to lose its county borough status (and thus its autonomous strategic planning powers). What is more, not only had the elections for the new Brighton District produced a council-elect which was only narrowly Conservative (thirty-one to twenty-eight) but also the new planning officer-elect had been Director of the Greater Brighton Structure Plan team. As we have seen, this team was in favour of a balanced growth for the town and whatever else might be said about the station proposals, nobody could pretend that they incorporated enough housing for the jobs that would be generated. The pro-development lobby was therefore involved in a race against time if they were to obtain the planning consent by 31 March 1974 when the new structure would take over responsibility.

But late in 1973 it became apparent that there was a flaw in the applicants' legal position; they did not have an Office Development Permit. In effect therefore their application was null and void. This was made clear in a letter written both to the Department of the Environment and the Town Clerk by the lawyer acting for the 'Save Brighton Station' campaign. In the absence of a *valid* development application (that is, an application accompanied by an ODP) the applicants could be seeking only a re-zoning of the site. But, said the letter, '. . . there is no provision in law to re-zone land as such'. Late in February 1974, the Department confirmed to Brighton the correctness of this view and simultaneously wrote back to the lawyer. This second letter simply pointed out that this was a matter between the Department and the local authority – an example of both the defensiveness of the bureaucratic mind and of the Department's attitude towards public participation in planning.

The pro-development lobby was left in some embarrassment. Early in March 1974, with only three weeks to go to the local government reorganization, Brighton Corporation applied to have the land re-zoned. The 'Save Brighton Station' campaign wrote to the Department a week later urging the Secretary of State not to agree to this. Late in March the minister rejected Brighton's last ditch attempt and, temporarily at least, the developer's cause was lost.

Some disquiet was subsequently expressed about the way in which the development application had been handled. As we have seen the application was invalid since no ODP was attached but it was numbered, and statutory notices were displayed as if it were in order. When the absence of an ODP became widely known, it was maintained that the application was an 'informal' one. Moreover it was suggested that it had foundered because the Secretary of State had been unwilling to accept the necessary departure from the old Development Plan zoning. This was by no means the only reason as we have seen.

The 'Save Brighton Station' campaign was well aware of the progress of events and on 22 March they wrote to the Brighton *Evening Argus*. They drew attention to the apparently desperate moves that were being made to facilitate the development and in view of the wide public concern they called upon the Council to explain more fully what was happening. Although the matter was indisputably of great interest to the people of Brighton, the letter was not published.

Late in 1974, at the time of writing, the issue is still in doubt. Following the unsuccessful move in March a seven-man 'ad hoc' committee was set up to renegotiate with British Rail. It was generally hoped (and the Housing and Planning Committees both agreed) that whatever uses emerged on the site there would be a substantial amount of housing and other community uses. In July 1974 the Chief Officers reported to the ad hoc group that an ODP for commercial offices was unlikely, but that nevertheless a powerful commercial incentive would be required if redevelopment were to be encouraged and that possibly non-commercial offices might be located here (such offices could be just as profitable to develop and would not require an ODP). The ad hoc committee of councillors (four Conservative and three Labour) has not yet made much progress with renegotiation. But late in November 1974 other informal talks got under way between British Rail and the chairmen of committees, plus officers, of Brighton, Hove and East Sussex (all the politicians in this group being Conservatives). Statements to the local press stressed the non-official and exploratory nature of these talks. But seasoned observers of the scene are in no doubt about their significance. The development lobby is on the march again, with what success time alone will tell.

Jubilee Street

The Jubilee Street site occupies about $5\frac{1}{2}$ acres of central land just to the north of the Royal Pavilion. Brighton Corporation have been quietly buying up plots in the area over a number of years and by 1964 they already owned more than half of the site which was occupied, in the main, by a mixture of small shops, houses, industrial premises, car parks and the town's ancient swimming baths. Late in that year a specially set up Joint Committee on Exhibition and Conference accommodation recommended that the Council should acquire the rest of the site by compulsory purchase and should declare it a Comprehensive Development Area. They proposed that a large exhibition hall and multi-storey car park should be built on the site together with a new library. In February 1965, the Planning Committee recommended that the scheme should be approved.

By 1967 there had been a change of heart. Because it was now clear that the demand for exhibition space was being met elsewhere in the town and that it was apparent that the government was unlikely to sanction loans for the particular uses Brighton had in mind, the scheme was abandoned. Nevertheless the Council decided to continue to acquire plots on the site as and when possible and by 1969 they owned 80% of the area. At this point the Council began to explore other possibilities. The Corporate Estates Committee noted:

Since the restrictions on capital expenditure by local authorities which have existed over the last five years have not yet been substantially eased and private enterprise being relatively free of the economic restraint imposed by the Government on municipal expenditure, your Committee feel it would be advantageous if an opportunity were given to private developers to make offers for developing the site, on the basis of a scheme incorporating some or indeed all of the Council's own requirements within the development of the area.

They therefore recommended that the site should be leased out to private developers. Thus an important relationship was established. At a time of cut-back in public expenditure local authorities will tend to farm out their development projects to private enterprise and seek, with varying degrees of enthusiasm, competence and conviction, to acquire the public facilities they need in return for the licence to make money which a planning consent represents.

Finally, in July 1972, the Corporate Estates Committee again brought proposals to the Council. In the meantime the Planning Committee had identified land uses they would like to see on the site. They included such amenities as a sports centre and swimming pool, a library, a youth centre, an arts centre, an exhibition hall, a conference hall, a museum, offices and housing. They suggested an overall space limit of 350,000 sq. ft, but the Corporate Estates Committee noted that since the redevelopment was a private one, and therefore needed to be 'viable economically':

This means, of course, that it would not be possible to incorporate in the development all the uses that have been considered and approved by the Planning Committee.

Instead:

... your Committee is satisfied that an appropriate balance between public and private requirements for this site could be made by the Corporation requiring only a new swimming pool and library as part of the development.

Noting:

... the desirability of encouraging office growth within Brighton in order to bring about increased employment and rateable value ...

(and thus directly contradicting all the advice they had been receiving from the professional planners) the Committee:

... therefore feels that a substantial part of this site can be made available for office development because of its central location and clearly this is the type of use that would encourage developers to join into partnership with the Corporation.

They therefore recommended a split between offices and housing, once the land for public uses had been earmarked, in the ratio two thirds to one third. It has subsequently been suggested that a re-allocation of some of the residential content to office use might take place. No one should have been surprised at these proposals despite their obvious inconsistency with the recommendations of the *Greater Brighton Structure Plan*; the writing had been on the wall from the point when it was agreed that the site should be leased out for private redevelopment. Cultural and sporting facilities are less profitable than offices.

The Corporate Estates Committee conceded that the normal practice was to invite a number of developers to submit schemes and tenders. But apparently informal discussions had already taken place. One developer, Star (Great Britain) Developers Ltd, was keen to 'help out' and it was clear that 'they would see eye to eye' with the Corporation. Since the committee 'is anxious that an early start should be made on the redevelopment because of the difficulties that will be experienced in the transfer of property on local government reorganization', and since advertising and tendering would consume 'valuable months', it was felt that competition could be dispensed with. Star, it was argued, were one of the largest development companies and '. . . would inevitably be strong candidates for any major development scheme . . .' But the Finance Committee was not impressed. They simply recommended '. . . that applications to develop this site be invited on the open market', and this was agreed.

A developer's brief was prepared by the Town Clerk and Borough Valuer. It declared that this was a unique opportunity 'to undertake a development which is capable of attracting both high prestige and profit . . .' The brief set out the required land uses as agreed in July 1972 (a library, a swimming pool, and of the remainder of the site one third residential and two thirds commercial) although schemes without a swimming pool were also invited. The lease was to be for 125 years, with a first rent review after twenty years and subsequent reviews at ten-year intervals, and developers were invited to submit schemes and make offers for the lease.

Four developers, including the previously front-running Star (G.B.) Developments, submitted schemes. These were considered by Corporate Estates Committee on 6 September 1973 and were given their first public airing in the local press on the next day. This gave just twenty days notice to the public (and to most councillors) before the full council meeting at which it was hoped the scheme would be approved. The committee recommended that the schemes submitted by County and District Properties Limited should be accepted. The successful scheme included a pool, eighty units of housing and 178,000 sq. ft of office space. In the report submitted with their financial offer, the developers referred to the offices as 'fully air-conditioned with carpeting and suspended ceilings'.

The Labour group were less than enthusiastic about the scheme and one of them proposed that the issue should be deferred for a month to give everyone more time to think about it (twenty days was seen as a little on the short side) and possibly to revive the idea of the Council itself developing the site, perhaps with a larger proportion of community facilities. The reported response of the chairman of the Finance Committee is interesting:

Where he thinks this council can raise this sort of money from I don't know. We aren't magicians. If he can whistle up this money then I'd like to see him afterwards. We need his knowledge.

As most councillors were probably aware the Council *is* going to have to find 'this sort of money' in the near future to improve the roads and services to the marina to enable the developers there to carry out an even larger scheme. But that is another issue.

The chairman of Corporate Estates, reportedly enthused about 'this exciting scheme' as '. . . a classic example of what could be done with a young team of officers keen on an idea . . .' and he remarked, quite accurately if not altogether wisely: 'I don't think any scheme has been brought in quicker than this one'.

When the financial details were released it was seen that the developers were offering an anual ground rent of £192,000 for the site. They were prepared to lease the library back to the Council for £69,000 a year and to give the swimming pool to the town. This 'gift' was headlined in the local press and the outcome seemed to be generally regarded as a triumph of negotiation. Criticism, or even more thorough questioning, of the financial arrangements might have been construed as ingratitude. This attitude is mistaken, as a rough reconstruction of the financial position will show.

The main money spinner in the scheme is the 178,000 sq. ft of offices. At a rental on completion of £3 per sq. ft (in view of the apparent building standards and the location it could soon be nearer £5) the annual rent revenue would be £534,000. Together with rental from the eighty flats (say £50,000) and the library (£69,000), the annual return should hardly be less than £650,000. The rent offered to the Council (fixed for twenty years) is £192,000 and this figure represents the residual once the annual cost of borrowing the capital to carry out the construction has been paid (see Chapter 1). This annual cost of around £450,000 represents, at a very rough guess, a loan of about £5 million which, one concludes, is the anticipated cost of the total work.

The significance of these calculations is that if one uses the assumptions appropriate to the pre-slump property market then it is possible to make some estimate of the asset creation involved. At pre-slump yield levels (see Chapter 1) a prime office building of this type might be worth between fifteen and eighteen times the annual rental. This would have placed the capital value on completion at between £8 million and £9.6 million *for the office component alone*. The difference between this value and the cost figure of £5 million worked out above, a difference of the order of £3 million to £5 million, represents an asset created for the developer by the action of granting him a planning consent. It is therefore hardly surprising that the town should get a swimming pool in return. This would probably cost much less than £1 million, or something like 20% to 25% of the value handed out with the planning permission – rather less of a bargain than one might have expected.

These calculations have had to be approximate because this sort of financial detail is not published and moreover few councillors appear to know about it. But the figures are entirely consistent with the levels of profit on completion, and on annual revaluation, that had recently been experienced by the developers concerned. The 1973 *Report and Accounts* of County and District Properties show upward revaluations of 15% to 30% over 1972 figures which is generally in line with trends in commercial rents over the year. Moreover a *Financial Times* report of 23 November 1973 notes that the company had acquired further development sites in prime locations on 'advantageous terms' and it specifically mentions the Brighton scheme. The report continues:

The acquisitions bring the overall value on completion of future developments in hand, subject to planning permission, to more than £85 million against a total cost of about £48 million.

Assuming that the developers do not operate less profitably in Brighton than elsewhere (and few would maintain that Brighton has been an unrewarding town for developers) then the rough calculations set out above are not unreasonable. In the conditions applying up to the end of 1973, the company was finding that the value of its completed developments exceeded the development costs in the ratio of about nine to five; an immediate return of 70% to 80%. At this rate of wealth creation it is doubtless expedient to boost one's image by distributing 'free' swimming pools.

The difficulties and uncertainties that stemmed from the sudden plunge from boom to slump between November 1973 and March 1974 caused a slow-down in the Jubilee Street redevelopment. Almost simultaneously, reorganization had produced a Brighton council which was almost evenly balanced politically and suggestions began to be made that the scheme should be rethought and that more community facilities should be included in the redevelopment.

The Chief Officers wrote a report which put forward other ideas. They noted that an increase in amenity uses would 'effectively exclude all commercial development from the site'. They also dwelt upon the cramped conditions under which various of Brighton's local government departments were working and they recommended that the development scheme already approved could be adapted to house a Civic Office Complex. This, they pointed out, would not conflict with the moratorium on further commercial office development. Moreover, the office space currently used in buildings along the seafront would, if vacated, free these sites for 'a major hotel development'.

In view of the national uncertainty in the property world a

director of County and District Properties wrote to the Chief Executive in June 1974 stressing that his company's interest in the development was undiminished despite the 'nasty set-back' in the property market. He hoped that the Chief Officers would continue to urge councillors to support the scheme especially in view of '... the poor and inefficient facilities at present enjoyed by the Council employees'. As a result, the Chief Executive wrote to the council's Lands Sub-Committee referring to the 'excellent and sustained' efforts of the developers in carrying out the work and especially in approaching the outstanding private owners of properties on the site. Success here would mean earlier completion '... without having to await the results of Public Inquiries etc ...' It is well known that such participatory devices cause delays, and therefore extra costs and it is obviously in the interests of the developers that the site be consolidated and cleared with minimum delay. In such circumstances it is particularly important that the legal rights of existing owners and tenants are safeguarded and that the progress of events is publicly monitored, if necessary by means of an inquiry.

Who Gains and Who Loses?

The gainers

Top of the list of gainers from the case studies reviewed come British Rail/Peachey Properties, and County and District Properties Ltd. If the property market returns to pre-1974 conditions, as seems likely unless some fundamental changes are made, they stand to make gains of the order of £5 million on completion of the schemes they are involved in, and this may be a gross underestimate. Next in the list of gainers come the professional facilitators of these developments. Architects, surveyors, lawyers, valuers, and estate agents are all richly rewarded for what are, in many cases, relatively simple tasks in the development process.

But beyond the actual projects, the whole pattern of development seems to benefit the better off. Offices that are 'fully airconditioned with carpeting and suspended ceilings' are probably excellent things in themselves but if we took an average of the

incomes of those who ended up working in them we should probably conclude that the benefits of comfortable working conditions
had reached upper income, rather than lower income, people.
Similarly, the users of luxury hotels and conference centres tend
to have above-average incomes (and/or expenses) and the notion
of using large areas of land at the station for car parks for the
convenience of these users, seems morally questionable in a town
desperately short of housing land. Indeed, the whole business of
investing large resources for the convenience of car-owners (in
roads and car parks for example) seems regressively redistributive since car-owners are, clearly, better off on average than non-
car-owners. So the general pattern of financial gain is clear, even
if, in view of the data deficiencies, the precise size of the gains
cannot be quantified.

The losers

There are a lot more of these and their loss can take many forms.
So closely inter-related are the workings of the urban system that
in most cases their loss is intimately related to, and a direct result
of, the developer's gain. Resources used to create luxurious offices
cannot be used for the competing task of providing more and
better housing. The overall housing shortage in the area was outlined earlier in the chapter and in addition to this many households live in very poor conditions. In some inner wards in
Brighton up to 77% of households are in the privately rented
sector and there is a heavy incidence of overcrowding and shared
dwellings. Only just over half these households have the exclusive use of an indoor toilet plus a bath and hot water system and
many families are living below statutory housing standards. The
deficiencies are considerable and they correlate with other social
problems.

This was shown by a recent study of the relationship between
local housing conditions and certain kinds of mental and physical
disorder. The study, which was carried out by Christopher Bagley, used housing data from the 1966 Census and roughly concurrent data on mental health, suicide and so on. The work refers
to much previous research on the same relationships and it sets
out to test the idea that

High rates of social pathology (crime, delinquency, suicide, mental illness and family problems) will tend to cluster together in areas which are high on indices such as overcrowding, poverty and adverse social conditions.

On the whole this relationship was amply demonstrated in Brighton. Psychiatric illness tended to occur most frequently in areas which were heavily overcrowded or which had a high proportion of furnished tenancies. High rates of depression, schizophrenia, alcoholism, severe personality disorder, affective psychosis, suicide and parasuicide all correlated strongly with the same housing variables. The incidence of most of these was most strongly marked in the inner wards of the town. The general picture is one of '. . . multiple pathology – mental illness, crime, and child welfare problems – emanating from wards in the central area of the city'. There is, of course, much evidence from elsewhere to support this statement. The loss it depicts is in terms not of money but of peace of mind.

It is notoriously difficult to be sure of the meaning of these results. The existence of a correlation by no means demonstrates that one thing causes the other and it would not be possible from these findings alone to argue that a rapid improvement in housing conditions in the central wards would solve all the problems. But it is part of all social workers' common knowledge that a high percentage of the problems they deal with stem from a housing difficulty of some kind. The problem may be overcrowding, bad conditions, insecurity, rising rents or impending eviction; in many cases it is the triggering mechanism which leads to a sequence of events which leave the family or individual impoverished; mentally, socially, or financially. This impoverishment could be drastically reduced, if not entirely eliminated, by the provision of a separate dwelling for every household that needed one. But such a course would mean using sites like the station and Jubilee Street in a socially beneficial, rather than a commercially optimal, way.

What Have been the Guiding Principles?

This chapter will be concluded by drawing out a few strands of meaning from the two case studies. Perhaps the first point to make in retrospect is that the pattern of thinking and decision-making by the majority group has been, in every sense, conservative. Everything that has happened is entirely consistent with age-old capitalist assumptions about the socially and economically appropriate use to which any particular urban site should be put. Thus, for example, the suggestion that the station site be used for housing those in greatest need was dismissed because 'the site is worth millions' and was therefore inappropriate for such a purpose.

The same principle applies to the Jubilee Street site, nearly all of which the Council own. It could have been used for a comprehensive mix of recreational and cultural facilities, together with some low-cost housing. Various reports coming to the Council through the 1960s indicate that this solution was quite widely favoured. Instead the property lobby wish to use it largely for offices which, by all the professional advice, are not only unnecessary but which will enormously add to the planning problems of the town and area. In exchange for giving the developers an opportunity to make a considerable profit (at least £3 million at a very low estimate) the town is ready to settle for a 'free' swimming pool. And the deal has been publicly presented as such a triumph of negotiation that the criticism that it needs from the Labour benches has been stifled lest it should appear that Labour councillors are opposed to Brighton's children having a nice new swimming pool. Again, the Conservatives have simply implemented the capitalist notion of maximizing private profit without sufficient regard to any wider accountancy which would include social costs.

An aspect of Conservative ideology that has been consistently in evidence is their eagerness to farm out development, where at all possible, to private enterprise. A variety of rationales has been offered. Private developers are competent to do the job (an insulting reflection on the town's officers appointed by the council itself); a contract to the lowest tenderer keeps down costs (although attempts were made to avoid competitive tendering in the Jubilee Street case); and only private enterprise has the capital resources to carry out the work (yet local authorities can raise loans in a variety of ways). It was even argued at the November 1973 meeting of the Council, just before the Tory group presented the fruits of the renegotiation with British Rail on the station as a triumph of financial *savoir-faire*, that the town did not have the expertise to run a public car park and that yet another contract should go to an outside organization. One can only conclude that a council that cannot make a profit out of a car park in a town like Brighton is likely to run into difficulties.

Another guiding principle has been evident from the case studies; reveal as little as possible and discourage public participation. There are numerous examples of this. The Jubilee Street scheme had just twenty days' public notice before going to the Council (although public interest in the fate of the site had been evident for a decade at least). The first press notice of the station development exhibition was on 8 November 1973, three days after the exhibition had closed. The same principle applies in the decision-making process itself. It is arguable that *all* councillors (not just the few on the relevant committee) should have complete financial details of development schemes. These details should include not only the rent or purchase price offered by the developer, but also the capital gain he expects to make. In fact there is no good reason (and the widespread anger that this information would induce is not a good reason) why the *public* should not know all these details. Local people who are on pensions or supplementary benefits, or who are 'holding the country to ransom' for an extra pound or so a week might find them interesting. And it is after all, *their* town that the developer is getting his profit from.

Finally, one can argue that the Council were making the fatal mistake of running the town as if it were a commercial operation. This is not altogether surprising since many of the councillors are businessmen, but it does explain the continuing prominence of the three previous principles. In practice it means maximizing growth, minimizing costs (especially on the rates) and allowing land uses to be determined by the highest bidder in the market. This approach, whatever its effectiveness in running a commercial venture has certain grave defects when applied to an urban system. Our criticisms are not made on humanitarian grounds, for it would probably be a waste of time to try to achieve any change in the pattern of decisions by instancing the privations suffered by the poor. The argument is rather that on *purely economic grounds* the pattern of decisions has been inept in at least two ways.

The first is that the accountancy base has been too narrow; the cost/benefit analyses that have been carried out (if any) have been so obsessed with measurable financial gains that they have omitted social costs and benefits which, although not easily measurable, must exert a tremendous weight on any urban system. This point can best be illustrated by reference to selected figures from the Summary of Requirements from the General Rate Fund on the Council's estimates for 1973–4:

Health	757,800	
Social Services	1,886,130	2,643,930
Education		7,978,180
Housing		319,150
Parks		528,310
Royal Pavilion, Museums and Libraries		381,330
Total spending from General Rate Fund		17,312,990

Over £2.6 million of the rates is spent on health and social services. Big items in this figure include health visiting, the prevention of illnesses services, and the residential care of children and the elderly. A large part of the need for these services must stem from inadequate housing, as the town's own Medical Officer of Health (Dr W. Parker) has pointed out:

Last year the number of youngsters sent for child guidance treatment in Brighton rose by 15% in comparison with the previous year, and the number of children assessed as maladjusted doubled.

Dr Parker blames the increase on tensions at home caused by overcrowding and said that these frictions could be removed by 'a proper and wider housing policy'. He said 'putting the problem to social workers is like putting a thumb on a leak which shouldn't be there in the first place'.

(Brighton *Evening Argus* 14 December 1973)

In any case one does not have to rely on the observations of experienced field workers and doctors alone; the study by Christopher Bagley, and all the research he quotes, demonstrates the link between poor housing and an increased impact on the social services. Education is the largest single item in the budget. To what extent is the effectiveness of this expenditure being diminished by illness, truancy or lack of interest that are related, in some way, to some family housing problem? If, say, only 10% of the health and social services cost relates directly to housing inadequacies and only 1% of the education spending is being wasted for the same sorts of reasons (and both may be massive underestimates) then the cost of the housing crisis is nearly £350,000 per year.

But the cost to be found from the rates of building new housing for 2,000 people on some of the most expensive land in Brighton (on the station site) was assessed by the Council's own officers to be only £132,000 per year. The implication is startling. At present the annual rate cost of housing is only £319,000 (a lot less than the cost to the rates of parks and the Royal Pavilion etc.). By increasing this it is quite clear that a big step could be made towards alleviating the present conditions. Massive savings might then be possible in the spending on the social support services. One would be following the sensible policy of building fences at the top of the cliff rather than providing an expensive fleet of ambulances at the bottom. But this would not be in the interests of the property lobby on the Council because the elimination of housing scarcity could easily lead to a fall in local rents and property values.

The second way in which Brighton, as an urban system, is being apparently mishandled is in its dealings with developers. The point has to some extent been stressed already, but in order to re-emphasize it, one further simple truth needs stating. *Brighton does not need developers but they need Brighton.* They cannot carry on their uniquely profitable trade without the planning consents which local authorities are empowered to give. The controlling group on Council are projecting the idea that efforts must constantly be made to 'attract' big developers and their clients. But on all rational grounds, Brighton needs more offices like it needs an earthquake; and the latter might in the end be less costly.

The town is in an immensely strong bargaining position. Sites are becoming increasingly scarce in central London and Croydon and developers are continually looking to attractive alternatives. In this situation the town could hold out for some real planning gain before giving the next consent – say 500 or 1,000 new houses. It is surprising that the apparently 'hard-nosed' politicians and officers who have undertaken the negotiations on behalf of the town are not fully aware of the strength of their position.

These, then, are the main arguments against the way that planning and development have been handled in Brighton in the last decade or so. The main case against the pro-development lobby is not that they are insensitive to the housing deprivation and social hardships that accompany their policies. It is not even the political odium they create among supporters and opponents alike by their methods. It is that they do not grasp the full complexity of the urban system. Their financial calculations leave out far too many social costs and relationships which, because not demonstrable on a profit and loss account, they find difficult to comprehend. They are, in a word, too narrow in their understanding. It is neither here nor there whether the town likes the men who have been running its affairs; a more significant question is whether it can afford them.

Chapter 6 What is Going Wrong?

We have seen from Chapters 1, 2 and 3 that money for property redevelopment comes almost entirely from financial institutions who accept premiums, contributions and deposits from millions of individuals. Having gathered these savings, and having become long-term debtors to society, the institutions are then free to use the funds in a manner which attempts to maximize returns within acceptable risk limits. In recent years up to 20% to 25% of this money has been used for the purpose of developing or speculating in property, and much of it has gone to finance office redevelopment. This has produced high rates of return for the institutions and developers since they can take the profit and rely on public agencies to meet the immense social costs that result (see Chapters 4 and 5). Society therefore allows the financial/development system to extract and use vast surpluses, to redistribute wealth and welfare, and to play the game according to its own rules.

It follows that our critique is not concerned primarily with deficiencies in the land-use planning system although, as we have pointed out, the system of land control does serve to push up values and profits. But the issue is much broader. Trading and speculating in property are some of the main activities of finance capital which is, itself, near the heart of the capitalist system. Thus capitalism, as a whole, rests heavily on the need for certain kinds of development to take place, and for property values to be maintained and increased. When high interest rates or the fear of government intervention cause property values to fall or look suspect, then finance capital's difficulties are compounded and a partial withdrawal from the development sector takes place. We argue that the process of creating and maintaining high property values has side-effects that are inevitably and invariably damaging to the interests of non-property-owners and especially to local low-income residents and workers. And a withdrawal of investment in slump periods does not help because it leads to a drastic reduction in all forms of development including housebuilding. It therefore seems that the well-being of the property lobby and the well-being of lower income urban residents and workers are mutually opposed. No amount of tinkering with the land-use planning system is going to resolve this deep structural contradiction of late capitalism.

From the previous two chapters it is possible to identify various adverse effects resulting from commercial redevelopment. These can be grouped under three headings; the effects on the housing and employment structures of the local areas affected, on the pattern of wealth distribution, and on the way in which certain national resources are being used. Since, at any given time, so much of our urban fabric is being renewed, it seems inevitable that when added up across the country, these effects must have a very significant impact on the economy as a whole.

The Effects of Commercial Redevelopment

On local employment, housing and living costs

The most evident effect of many large-scale redevelopments is an over-rapid and insensitive transformation in the social and employment structure of the areas affected. These two aspects are of course inextricably related since the social structure of an area, and to some extent its age/sex balance, is powerfully conditioned by the spread of jobs available within easy commuting range. Young and Willmott's classic study of Bethnal Green revealed, among other things, the organic inter-relationship between social and employment structure in an inner suburb of London not too dissimilar from North Southwark.

Such areas, and towns like Brighton, evolve socially and economically all the time and it would be futile to argue in favour of policies that imply some kind of social and economic 'preservation order' on what are, in effect, living organisms. This critique focuses therefore not on the *fact* of change but on the *process* of

135

change and on the social and economic effects that are felt when the rate of change exceeds some level defined by the needs of people who may have lived in the area for a generation or more. These needs can be easily understood. Typically, in the local workforce, there may be a number of manual workers nearing retirement while their children and grandchildren may be leaving schools in the area and seeking some form of non-manual employment. Many of these young people might prefer secretarial or clerical work and in the unforced evolution of areas like North Southwark and Brighton one might look for the gradual replacement of factory work-space with office work-space. A planning policy based on people's needs would attempt to foresee this slow change in the profile of job needs and would arrange for physical redevelopment to occur in harmony with it.

There is, of course, no relationship at all between this ideal approach and what is actually happening in the case study areas or in many others like them. North Southwark lost about 17,000 manufacturing jobs between 1967 and 1972 and the process of job loss, due partly to industrial closures brought about by asset stripping, has continued unabated since then. What will emerge instead is 20,000 to 30,000 office jobs. No one is pretending that laid-off manual workers in their fifties and sixties are suddenly going to become clerks and typists. The office desks will be manned principally by people who will commute daily from the outer suburbs or who will move into suitably 'gentrified' property in the borough. It is perfectly clear that the timescale of this massive employment transformation is geared to causes other than the gently evolving employment needs of the locality. It is equally clear that a rapid employment transformation of this scale will have many ripple effects, not least on the price of housing in the area and on the type of residential redevelopment that is judged appropriate by developers and planners alike. The effect these changes will have on long-established life-styles and patterns of community life is a matter which appears to be taken seriously only by the groups opposing the development.

The social and economic transformations brought about by redevelopment in Brighton are less dramatic in scale but show the same tendencies. The widespread incidence of 'gentrification', the very low priority given to local authority housing, and the loss of over 700 units of rented accommodation between 1961 and 1971, all add up to a situation in which low-income people are being squeezed out of the area. By contrast, every encouragement has been given to the development of new office complexes, hotels, conference centres and the marina with its proposed array of high-cost flats. Many commentators, of all political shades, have pointed out the likely disastrous consequences of this conspicuously ill-balanced pattern of evolution. In fact the evidence, in the form of spiralling accommodation costs, residential pressure on surrounding areas and a growing shortage of essential but lower-paid workers, is so pervasive that it need hardly be detailed.

Again, as in the case of North Southwark, the process is one of change in a direction, and at a rate, which clearly does not meet the essential needs of local people. These needs would be partly met by using the Brighton station site for low-cost housing. Such a course would contribute to the reduction of housing stress in two ways; by housing 1,500 to 2,000 people and by *not* producing several thousand more office workers who, together with their families, will constitute an extra demand pressure on the housing stock and social services of the area.

On wealth inequality

If the process of urban redevelopment is approached from the viewpoint of its redistributive effects on the pattern of wealth holding (and here wealth is defined broadly to include environmental considerations), the key question to ask about any plan or scheme is 'who gains and who loses?' Over the past few years it has been pointed out many times that planning decisions can never have a distributionally neutral effect. Some people gain as a result and some people lose. Characteristically the gains are large, accrue to a limited number of people and can be quantified in money terms. The losses impinge on many more people and can take several forms, some of which are non-quantifiable. The assertion that the net effect is regressively redistributive, that is to say that it helps the rich at the expense of the poor, rests on the invariable circumstance that in any redevelopment one can think of the gainers as better off than the losers to start with.

As was made clear in the case studies, the gainers from a re-development scheme in normal economic circumstances are the owners of the freeholds and/or leaseholds of the land concerned, the professional facilitators, the developers, and the investing or lending institutions. These institutions, whether banks, pension funds or insurance companies, are simply channelling the deposits, contributions or premiums of millions of individual savers. They will frequently argue, when a public relations drive seems advisable, that the profits are thus returned to the ordinary man in the street. This argument is, at best, a half-truth.

The ownership interest in superannuation fund assets appears to be extremely unequally spread between different income groups. From government actuarial returns and personal income surveys it seems evident that the total tax concession on employees' contributions to occupational pension schemes £155m in 1970–71) is very unequally divided. It has been calculated that those earning less than £1,000 receive an average of £1.1 of tax concession per year and those earning over £5,000 an average of £42.7 (1970–71). From these figures, and making allowance for several necessary adjustments, it has been suggested that the pattern of *ownership* in pension fund assets may be as follows:

income range	% of population	share of total superannuation funds owned
Less than £1,000	32	3%
£1,000 to £1,999	48	11%
£2,000 to £4,999	18	31%
£5,000 and over	2	55%

The total assets of these funds in 1972 amounted to £12,000 million. Even allowing for possible inaccuracies in deducing the ownership pattern from the distribution of tax relief, the figures suggest that a highly disproportionate share of this total sum may be owned by the highest income 2% of the population.

The same general degree of inequality may also apply to the pattern of rights to total life assurance funds. The average amount of tax relief on premiums seems to range from £4.8 per year for those earning less than £1,000 to £102.8 per year for those earning over £5,000. It has been calculated that this implies

the following distribution of participation in life assurance
funds:

income range (pa)	% of population	share of total interest in life assurance funds
Less than £1,000	32	6%
£1,000 to £1,999	48	10%
£2,000 to £4,999	18	27%
over £5,000	2	57%

Again, over half the total interest in these funds may be owned
by the richest 2% of the population.

The ownership of equity stocks and shares and unit trust
funds, including those in companies and funds benefiting from
redevelopment profits, is similarly biased in favour of the
wealthy. Evidence submitted to the Page Committee on National
Savings showed that at the end of 1971, 46% of unit trust holders
were in occupational categories A and B (managers, administra-
tors and professionals). Only 5% of holders were semi-skilled or
unskilled workers. In terms of direct holdings of stocks and
shares, as opposed to unit trusts, it appears that we have moved
little, if at all, from the situation in 1954 when the richest 1%
owned about 81% of all company shares owned by individuals,
executors and trustees. Although it is true that institutional
holders of shares have increased their proportion of total securities from one fifth to one third, these institutions, as we have
seen, largely represent the rich investors in disguise.

The implications of these figures are obvious. The massive
profits made from property redevelopment (in all except slump
periods), are returned partly to the investing and lending institutions and, through them, to the contributors to the pension funds
and the holders of life insurance policies. These are the *You* of
the full-page advertisements of such interests as the Property
Progress Group. But the advertisers must be aware of the unequal pattern of ownership in the investing institutions and in
the stock market. The profits from property redevelopment go
back overwhelmingly to the wealthy and a very high proportion
go back to the richest 1% or 2%. The statement made in the advertisements of the Property Progress Group that this represents

'. . . a fair share of profit for all the people' is not only misleading; it is actually untrue. There is a proportion of people who do not participate *in any way* in financing redevelopment since they hold no private insurance or pension rights at all. These people are, of course, the lower paid and perhaps that is why the Property Progress Group regards their nil return as a fair share.

There are various financial and environmental losses to be set against this pattern of gain. As the case-study chapters show, the loss can take many forms, depending upon the particular way in which redevelopment affects the household. The first possibility, and the least severe in impact, is that the household is able to retain its existing home and job(s) but that large-scale office redevelopment occurs in the immediate vicinity. This is likely to lead to an increase in local rent levels as a result of the growth in local demand for accommodation stemming partly from incoming groups with the economic resources to bid up rents. The same effect may be felt in the prices of commodities in the shops. The effect on prices may be aggravated by the progressive removal of the old-established 'corner shop' structure of retailing. This may lead to a reduction in local competition between the shops that are left and a consequent risk of higher prices. It may also lead to the progressive removal of key services such as pharmacists. All these effects are very evident in North Southwark.

It will be argued by the planners and developers that the various redevelopment schemes will include new shops, with possibly even a bigger total square footage than exists at present. What they fail to point out is that there may be a period of five years or more between the loss of shops and their replacement, that the new shops will exist in large centres in a relatively nucleated pattern (thus increasing average distances from homes to shops) and that the rent levels, and the profile of demand generated by the office workers who will be their prime users, will effectively preclude most of the existing traders in the area from renting the new retail space. One need only look at the pattern of retailing already building up in the new shops by London Bridge Station to see an example of this tendency.

Another possible effect of redevelopment is that land which was previously used residentially is re-zoned for other uses. This naturally means that people are uprooted and forced out of the area. If they are owner-occupiers this usually means receiving compensation on a scale which often makes a further purchase difficult or impossible. If they are council tenants it means, in most cases, a rent increase since the accommodation they are moved into is likely to be newer, and therefore more expensive, than that which they were used to. On top of this there is the extra expense of refurnishing and the social disruption which is involved in any residential move. The forced move may also result in disruption of long-standing arrangements for the daily journey to work and the longer the move, the greater the potential cost of commuting back to the place of work. These are costs which many people choose to incur in situations where choice is possible; in a move forced by redevelopment there is no choice.

Another possibility is that redevelopment will lead to the loss of the local job that provides all or most of the household's income. As we have seen, this has occurred in many thousands of cases already in North Southwark, mostly as the result of asset-stripping. The ex-employee has only a limited range of choice in this situation since it is obviously unlikely that similar work can be found locally, in view of general trends in the area. If he is nearing pensionable age he may be able to retire prematurely, which means a drop in income. If he is much younger he may be obliged to get work much further afield, which means an increase in the time and cost of getting to work. A final possibility is that the family loses both home and job and has to move out of the area altogether. This is the most disruptive of all and it leads to a number of financial and other costs as the family seeks to re-establish itself in a new area and to find a new job, new accommodation, new schools and new friends.

When the question 'who gains and who loses?' is examined from all these points of view, it is difficult to see how those responsible for redevelopment can be losing (except in the temporary and short-term conditions of a property slump), and equally difficult to see how the vast majority of the local people affected can be gaining. After redevelopment the area may *look* more glossy and presentable and the planners and developers may even feel they have 'solved' the area's problems. But, in fact, they have not solved them at all; they have exported them. Large-scale shifts of wealth and welfare have resulted and the people who were there at the beginning have either been forced elsewhere (largely at their own expense) or have had to commit a far higher proportion of their probably below average income to pay for the necessities of shelter, food, clothing and transport to work. The profits of the scheme have not gone back to them but have been absorbed into the wealth of those who already own land, leases, property shares, or insurance and pension rights.

The implication is inescapable; the whole process of urban redevelopment is regressively redistributive and it is contributing, possibly on a very significant scale, to wealth inequality. The national debate about the processes that perpetuate wealth inequalities and the 'cycle of deprivation', a debate conducted so far largely in terms of rates of taxation and death duty, needs to be extended to include the redistributive effects, both financial and environmental, of the urban redevelopment process.

On the use of national resources

The argument here is that heavy investment in office redevelopment, especially in the congested south-east, may well be a misuse of resources, given that various alternative forms of investment are possible. The idea of misuse is laden with value judgements and cannot sensibly be discussed at all except in the context of a generally agreed set of aims. Insofar as one can detect national aims from the statements of leading politicians it seems that these include the growth of our productive capacity, the achievement of better industrial relations, and the solution of our major domestic crises which, in most people's view, would include the wealth inequality situation and the housing shortage.

We have already argued that the urban redevelopment process *increases* wealth inequalities and there is little we can say about its bearing on industrial relations (although one can hardly believe that widely publicized multi-million pound-property profits are a factor leading to industrial peace and the moderation of wage claims). The arguments in this section will therefore concentrate on the inappropriateness of present property investment patterns to the achievement of growth in our productive capacity and to the solution of our housing crisis.

The housing argument is the easier one to make. With a million or more people homeless and about a fifth of the total housing stock below legal standards, it hardly bears repeating that Britain needs more housing. It is also evident that more offices are needed as the nation's employment structure tends to produce more and more office jobs. What is conspicuously missing is any rational and socially responsible means of determining in what proportions new housing and new offices should be added to the national stock. In practice the decisions that produce new development or redevelopment, are based on considerations of short-term finacial gain and not on a saner long-term view of society's needs. In recent years this has produced a rapid switch of resources away from housebuilding and towards office development (see Chapter 1).

This general argument can be supported in detail by the case studies dealt with in Chapters 4 and 5. The Brighton station issue provides a perfect example. Central government had issued a clear directive to the nationalized industries to release land wherever possible for local housing needs and, as everyone knows, there is a severe shortage of development land in Brighton. The local press has been carrying editorials on the issue for a number of years and local councillors of both parties had been agonizing about it for at least as long; in fact at the November 1973 meeting of Brighton Council, one Conservative councillor actually placed his hand somewhere in the region of his heart as he spoke about the difficulties faced by young couples trying to find a home. To complement all this, at least three official reports had been presented to the Council stressing the excessive rate at which new office floorspace was being added to the town and detailing the difficulties that this was causing.

Despite these circumstances, when the time came to make a decision between a complex of offices and commercial uses on the one hand and the possibility of low-cost housing for up to 2,000 people on the other, the crocodile tears were replaced by the imperatives of the market place. The site was too central, and thus too valuable, to be used for the highly unprofitable purpose of housing people. Despite the efforts of opposition groups, commercial principles prevailed. The same general line of argument was used in Southwark where attempts to get south-bank land opposite the City zoned for housing met with no success because 'riverside land is not suitable for family housing'. A trip up and down the Thames by boat will reveal plenty of riverside housing. The real reason for the refusal was that the land was too near the City and thus had too great a commercial potential.

The argument that recent property development patterns have been detrimental to the long-term growth in productive capacity of the national economy is more difficult to substantiate. It rests upon a number of intuitively made judgements since, strange as it may seem, there appears to be no research aimed at determining the best mix of new building types required in order to maximize growth in the Gross National Product. Such research would, of course, be extremely complex but in the absence of the guidelines it would produce, it is evident that the mix of square footage that is added to the nation's built space year by year is determined largely by the relative rates of return on different kinds of development.

In the absence of research on this issue, dialogue can proceed only in terms of assertion. The view of the commercial office development lobby is summed up in a report by the estate agents Debenham, Tewson and Chinnocks who asserted that the slow growth of the British economy is as much conditioned by the shortage of modern office space in the south-east as by any other factor. Any ban on office growth 'can only aggravate the economic inefficiencies of the nation' and 'good housing for all' stems basically from 'increased business efficiency'.

More general arguments along the same lines were advanced in *The Times* Special Report dated 9 October 1974 on invisible earnings. This pointed out that of the net surplus of £2,100 million on invisible trade, the City of London contributed £704 million. Of this, £374 million came from insurance transactions, which may help to explain the political significance of the insurance lobby. It will no doubt be argued that this kind of activity requires increasing amounts of centrally located office space to accommodate it.

But on closer inspection the same report provides much evidence for an alternative view. It expresses a general concern that the invisibles surplus could fall in the future since its growth is dependent on the growth of visible trade (that is, trade in actual goods). Furthermore the size of the invisibles surplus could be threatened by the extent of foreign investment in Britain, mostly by oil-producing countries, which will in time lead to large debit items in the form of interest payments. Therefore, for two reasons, future invisible earnings may be endangered by a lack of *domestic* investment in our industrial capacity to manufacture goods for export. It is only by investment of this kind that our invisibles surplus will be built up on the basis of tangible exports and that we can avoid heavy interest repayments to overseas sources of borrowing. It is therefore arguable that the absolute priority is to direct investment into our manufacturing plant and that the 'invest in offices for national prosperity' argument is a piece of special pleading by the finance capital/development lobby. Rather significantly, the same report commented that due to lack of '. . . heavy-handed legislation and central bank control' the City has a 'flexibility' to be found nowhere else. Perhaps the flexibility is actually a licence to serve sectional interests rather than national needs.

There are various other counter-arguments to the property lobby's assertions. The consequence of committing resources to office building rather than to housing is a housing crisis which in itself must be extremely costly to the nation. The consequence of investing resources in producing working space where pieces of paper are endlessly shuffled, recorded, typed on, pored over and filed is that these resources cannot be invested in producing working space (and plant, tools and equipment) which actually produce things that people need. And where the paper work is generated by activities of such dubious social worth as advertising, public relations, unnecessarily complicated legal transactions and the like, the ultimate wastefulness seems more and more apparent.

Apart from this it seems odd to construct, say, a 100,000 sq. ft block in Central London to accommodate 700 office workers in space costing £15 per sq. ft per year when at least half of them are probably typists, junior clerks, telephonists or underemployed secretaries. Modern communications technology allows these tasks to be carried on hundreds of miles away in less crowded regions where the consequence of building the office block would be to solve a local employment need and not to aggravate a local housing crisis. Office space in such a location might cost perhaps £3 per sq. ft to the user. Can it really be maintained that a typist in the one location is worth five times as much to the national economy as a typist in the other? It seems doubtful.

Another counter-argument to that of the development lobby is that sometimes new office space is built to replace older offices on the same site; thus the total increment to the nation's office space is less than the total of new space created. The older offices, while no doubt less efficient than the new, could often have lasted another decade or so in view of the nation's needs to use all possible resources for development tasks of the highest priority. The decision to replace them owes nothing to these broader considerations. Equally, where newly created office space is kept empty after completion, as happens in a small but significant proportion of cases, this too represents a waste of scarce resources from a national point of view.

In view of the lack of research on the best national use of development resources, we do not claim that Debenham, Tewson and Chinnocks are completely wrong. Nor do we claim for our arguments the degree of certainty they seem to feel about theirs. But it does seem clear that if no controls are exerted, the pattern of development will be based on relative profitability levels. This situation is currently likely to produce a lot of new offices, hotels and leisure complexes, a fair amount of new shopping complexes and industrial buildings, and a small amount of new housing. It will also produce a disproportionately large share of development for the more congested regions.

Obstacles to Change

The planning and development system, like many other aspects of the establishment can be likened to a jelly; if you kick it, it flops back into place. As a preliminary to bringing about the radical overhaul necessary to alter its shape, we must identify the main impediments to change. At least three of these can be set out; the inertia that pervades the planning system, and especially the thinking of its senior members; the virtual non-participation of the local population in planning decisions; and the gradual withdrawal of central government as a financier, and therefore as an overseer, of development.

The key point about the planning system is that it is made up of bureaucratic organizations. Much has been written about bureaucracy. Max Weber identified precision, reliability and efficiency as the main attainments of a bureaucracy and he characterized bureaucratic man as methodical, prudent and disciplined. Attributes such as vision, personal relationships, non-rational or emotional involvements or willingness to engage the public in discussion are absent or poorly developed because they tend to detract from the main aim of predictability of response. According to various authors, bureaucracy also tends to see means as ends; the rules tend to become symbolic absolutes not devices to help attain a set of goals.

Veblen introduced the idea of the bureaucrat's 'trained incapacity', that is

. . . that state of affairs in which one's abilities function as inadequacies or blind spots. Actions based upon training and skills which have been successfully applied in the past may result in inappropriate responses *under changed conditions*. (Original author's emphasis.)

Furthermore, '. . . under new conditions . . . the very soundness of the training may lead to the adoption of wrong procedures'. (Quoted in Merton.) We feel that this analysis, and the idea of 'trained incapacity', applies perfectly to the planning system. The 'new conditions' stem from the growing realization, based on the work of such people as Gans and Harvey, that land-use planning can no longer be primarily concerned with technical and physical considerations. Planning is a powerful means of conditioning social perceptions and of redistributing tangible wealth. But the professional training planners receive has not yet fully come to terms with this reality and it may be a decade or so before it does. The educational programmes are, of course, strongly conditioned by the body of planning law which is so far totally insensitive to the emerging understanding of the full social implications of major planning decisions.

From this brief account of the nature of bureaucracy, it follows that it will be some time before radical, or even innovative, thinking begins to be noticed among senior planners. Chief planning officers, many of whom were trained in fields as socially barren as engineering and surveying, are inherently unlikely to take a far-reaching view of social needs in the urban system. They may, especially if ambitious and recently appointed, come in full of ideas on how to short-cut the system and assemble a structure plan in world record time (as in the case of East Sussex), but such aims are unlikely to be helpful in focusing attention on the needs of the less privileged and articulate of those being planned for (or, perhaps more accurately, against). The same comments also apply to many local authority architects, surveyors and, especially, treasurers.

The main reason for this is that, as Ralph Miliband has argued, government officials are '. . . expected to dwell within the spectrum of thought of which strong conservatism forms one extreme and weak "reformism" the other'. They are likely to perceive the 'national interest' or the 'community interest' in terms '. . . congruent with the long-term interest of capitalism'. These circumstances have a number of significant implications. Chief officers and civil servants are likely to take a conservative line on many, if not most, planning issues. They will frequently be successful in impressing this line on politicians, many of whom will be intimidated by the apparent technical expertise of the advice or by the detail of the presentation. Chapter 3 has set out a number of ways in which this conservatism, often based on the ever-present possibility that the recommendations may need to be defended at a planning inquiry, will manifest itself. Official account will be taken only of arguments on strict planning grounds, that is, on grounds recognized by the planning legislation and not on arguments based on the size of the profit involved in a proposal or on its broader social consequences for the area. For example, at the inquiry concerning the Morgan Crucible site in Battersea, the argument that the area needed low-cost, not luxury, housing was ruled out of order on the grounds that the final cost of the housing was not a planning matter; a conspicuous example of the law's absurdity. Recommendations or evidence to an inquiry tends to be set out in language which its authors may feel is careful and circumspect but which most of us would call just plain muzzy.

As the Town and Country Planning Association itself has pointed out, many planning officers are unwilling to establish working relationships with local activist groups and in the two areas studied in this book instances have occurred where senior officers have discouraged more junior planners from actively assisting community groups. Senior planners also tend to be reactionary in their response to proposals for which there is no precedent, such as the attempts by Christopher Booker and Benny Gray to get approval for a non-profit-making scheme in Camden which would have greatly benefited the housing situation in this borough. In all these respects the system is conforming to Weber's bureaucratic 'model'.

Senior local government officers are not only bureaucrats, they also tend to be pragmatists. In planning and development situations they are subject to pressures generated by the development lobby which are based entirely on a capitalist logic and to other pressures from the councillors, their notional 'masters', which in many cases are not too dissimilar. There is often every reason, on pragmatic grounds, to produce advice which looks 'independent' but which is in fact a technical rationalization of the outcome which would have occurred anyway. In so doing they may achieve limited aims of their own, for example building up a close relationship with powerful councillors or guiding through a big redevelopment scheme. From a career point of view all these ends are important, especially if the officer has aspirations to move from local government to a more lucrative position in the local business hierarchy.

One result of the general conservatism which pervades most planners' thinking is that their view of the appropriate configuration of land uses in the city tends to rationalize the view held by the operators of the private land market. Thus land near the centre of the city is tacitly assumed to be appropriate for 'central area uses' which is actually an official category on land-use maps. This perpetuates a vision of the city which dates back beyond medieval, and even Graeco–Roman, times; a vision of a blob of high-density commercial uses at the centre with other uses arranged concentrically outwards. The inevitability of this pattern which was given academic respectability in the work of Burgess and Alonso, has recently been questioned in radical new urban designs like Runcorn New Town. Nevertheless old habits die hard. Thus the Brighton station site was officially valued at £3 million (it had verbally been valued a few weeks earlier by the same official at about half this figure) even in the absence of any consent as to use because it was *assumed* that land in this location would naturally go for 'central area uses'. On a much larger scale, it has been assumed for a long time that North Southwark, just across London Bridge from the City, would eventually be redeveloped largely for such uses. It has been shown how this assumption led to industrial closures, asset-stripping, dereliction and the eventual approval of the strategy plan that incorporated the land-use zoning that the property lobby had been relying on all along. Both in Southwark and Brighton the process has all the attributes of a self-fulfilling prophecy based on a model of the city that goes back several thousand years to a quite different technological era. The model survives mostly, one suspects, because it maximizes the profit that can be made under the present system of property development.

The planning system's assumptions about central area uses is reinforced by the government financing arrangements for local authority land purchases. The Department of the Environment has to sanction the purchase of land for housing as the funds come out of 'key sector' finance. A given amount of money could purchase a small area of central land or a much larger area of suburban land (because of the land value gradient). A local authority might therefore expect to have to argue the case quite forcefully if it wished to acquire central land which, because of nearby office developments and the assumptions referred to previously, had acquired a very considerable 'hope' element in its market value.

Public non-participation in planning

Much has been written recently on the question of public involvement in planning decisions and there is no space here to develop the kind of detailed critique which, we believe, is now overdue. But it may be helpful to list various ways in which fundamental changes can be made to the social and economic structure of an area, and thus to the life-style of many thousands of people, as a result of planning processes which according to law require little or no public participation.

The participation procedures for structure and local plans are fairly clearly set out and before approving a plan the minister must be satisfied that the letter of the law (if not its spirit) has been observed. But the extent to which *amendments* to structure and local plans need to go through a consultation procedure is not yet clear. Informal non-statutory plans, such as strategy plans or informal local plans are not closely defined in law and carry with them no statutorily defined procedure for consultation. The only obligation is that the minister should be 'satisfied' that consultation has occurred. Since most of what is happening in Southwark is in the context of such a plan it is clear that non-statutory planning is a good way of avoiding the delay and trouble involved in obtaining a comprehensive view of the public's attitude.

Urban areas can also be radically affected as a result of designation as an 'action area', or a 'general improvement area' or as a 'conservation area'. Very often the effect in the latter two cases is for the housing costs in the area to rise, with the consequent partial squeezing out of long-standing low-income residents. The law in this case (the 1969 Housing Act) speaks in terms of having 'some idea' of the attitude of the people in the area before designation. The act specified that the authority should 'bring the action they propose to take to the attention of the local residents'. These weakly worded obligations offer *some* safeguard whereas 'gentrification' proceeding in a piecemeal fashion, with or without improvement grants, can radically transform an area in several years without requiring *any* prior consultation with the local residents. Equally, an asset-stripper can acquire a factory or a group of shops, close them down and put people out of work, and then clear the site ready for redevelopment without any obligation even to seek planning permission let alone to consult the workers or tenants in the premises. Another way of effectively disenfranchising the public is to obtain a planning permission for one set of plans and gradually to change them into something quite different. This tactic is being tried out on a surprisingly large scale in the case of the Brighton Marina. This list of the loopholes in the law concerning public participation is by no means complete. A more comprehensive study of this subject is needed.

In the context of these general remarks, it is instructive to review the history of public participation in the case of Southwark and Brighton. As Chapter 4 makes clear, it was the *Draft Strategy Plan for Southwark's Thames-side* published in April 1971, that formally spelt out the general expectations that a vast office component would be allowed in the redevelopment of the area. This draft plan, drawn up in some haste and in the context of considerable pressure from the development lobby, was produced in limited numbers. The council did not arrange any public meetings nor did they consult any local organizations, unions or institutions about the content or implications of the plan. Between 1971 and 6 March 1973, when the revised *Strategy Plan* itself was produced, the Council undertook no surveys on these matters. It was arranged that the Council would vote on the plan on 25 July 1973, thus restricting the consultation period to about twenty weeks. About a third of this period passed before the first news about the public information 'campaign' was printed in the *South London Press* on 20 April. A public meeting was arranged and advertised in the local press *three days* in advance. In the face of criticisms about lack of publicity, the Council promised to advertise the subsequent public meetings with door-to-door leafleting and press announcements. These promises were not kept, even in the areas where it was proposed to pull houses down, and little attempt was made to involve local organizations, shopkeepers, unions or residents.

As a result of this poor publicity, most of the public meetings attracted only a handful of people. The meetings themselves were obviously designed to 'sell' the plan and not to engage the public in a dialogue. It was never made clear which, if any, aspects of the plan were negotiable; no official records of public comments were kept and there was no official response to criticisms and questions raised by the public. In addition, doubt was cast on the credibility of local groups opposing the plan. Thus the meetings (which were the only consultation devices used) failed both to inform the public, because of derisory advance publicity, and to act as an effective sounding board of local opinion. Looking at the sequence of events, no one could conclude that the Council sincerely wished to achieve either of these two aims. Yet the re-development schemes that the plan legitimized, add up to perhaps the largest single land use transformation to occur in London since the Great Fire of 1666.

Compared to non-participation of this magnitude, events in Brighton were less dramatic. The planning application to re-develop the Jubilee Street site was given the bare twenty days publicity required by law even though it contained proposals which will radically affect a large site in central Brighton and which affect large public facilities such as the library and the town's main swimming pool. The likely rate of financial return and asset creation to the developers, and the relationship of this profit to the 'benefits' being offered to the town, is obviously a matter on which there should have been the widest public debate. Instead, far from being publicized in any effective way, it was clear that only a small handful of councillors, let alone the general public, fully understood the details of the deal with the developers. When questioned about it by a Labour councillor at the November 1973 meeting of the Council, one of this handful replied with a mixture of bluster, unnecessary mystification, and semi-veiled insult about the questioner's capacity to comprehend the issue. Such a response can only strengthen the suspicion that public debate on the financial details of the scheme was not viewed as desirable. Yet if the Council's negotiators were pleased with the arrangements they had made with the developers why would they not welcome a full public understanding of the financial details?

The attitude of the Department of the Environment towards several Brighton issues has also been clearly against public participation. Their cool reaction to the letter sent by the Save Brighton Station group concerning the status of the planning application to re-zone land was very revealing. Even more curious was the Department's letter to the Brighton Society explaining why they would not be sending a representative to an open meeting on the question of the routing of a proposed trunk road through the town. This read in part:

Our experience has shown that public meetings are not a good way of getting information across to people as the floor tends to be dominated by protest groups on these occasions and our officials are then put in the invidious position of being convenient Aunt Sallys for abuse.

This, on reflection, seems a quite astonishing statement to make. It contains within it the paternalistic notion that the main purpose of participation is for the government to 'get information across'; that protest groups are not a legitimate means of public comment; and that 'our officials' must be protected from any adverse comment.

Given this kind of attitude in Whitehall, and the highly selective reporting of planning issues that has been evident in the local press, it is obvious that the battle to achieve effective public participation in planning decisions will be a long and bitter one.

The withdrawal of central government

As Chapter 3 has shown, central government plays a complex, powerful and changing role in the process of land development and redevelopment. Devices that have been used to regulate this process have included a wide range of fiscal measures, physical controls such as ODPs and IDCs, planning acts that specify the types of plans within which development should occur and finally mechanisms such as public inquiries and appeals for adjudicating upon the most obvious cases of conflict.

Chapter 3 pointed to a number of defects in the view that central government is always willing and able to exercise an overriding influence on local development outcomes. For example, if no centrally approved structure plan yet exists, there is no obvious way (except at an inquiry or on appeal) that the minister can directly influence events. Equally, if proposals are being considered in the context of a non-statutory strategy plan the scope for ministerial intervention seems limited as does the scope for public participation (since no statutory consultation procedure has to be followed). In fact the greater the gap between what planning authorities *ought* to have produced in the way of formal long-term plans and the amount of such planning documents that they actually *have* produced, then the greater the scope for planning decisions that are based more on ad hoc considerations and the interests of developers than on a centrally approved growth pattern for the area. The size of the gap can be judged from the fact that few, if any, authorities had met all their obligations under the 1947 planning act (which required development plans to be drawn up and regularly revised) by the time the 1968 act was passed. And now in 1975, seven years later, hardly any of the Structure Plans called for in that act have been formally approved.

There is another way in which central government may be losing touch not just with the practicalities of decision-making but also with the real nature of the conflict over land use. Ministries responsible for environmental planning have always been concerned primarily with the purely physical and land-use aspects of proposals; they always have been, and still are, most interested in physical planning. But local people and activist groups all over the country are not burdened with this bureaucratic and legalistic lack of vision. They see that physical planning necessarily implies social planning and that under the cover of the technical appraisals some very political decisions about priorities and resources are being made. Thus every time the Department of the Environment, often in the person of an inspector at an inquiry, rejects arguments based on considerations such as the implications of a proposal for rents and living costs in the area, so it becomes correspondingly more obvious that officialdom has missed the point. And the more evident it becomes to people in general that the issues are social and political in nature, the less notice they are likely to take of a formal system that clings to an environmental and technical basis for decision-making. Unless changes occur in planning law to take account of the arguments that groups are increasingly tending to advance, then more and more direct action of some sort or another is bound to occur.

Apart from all this, central government has emasculated itself as a force in planning over the last thirty years by its withdrawal as the chief lender to local authorities. After the war, as shown in Chapter 3, the Public Works Loan Board provided the vast majority of all local authority loans at favourable rates of interest. The government was therefore well placed to influence the way in which the money was spent and it could, if it chose, exert heavy pressure on authorities to acquire land for necessary social purposes and to enlarge their public housing programme.

Authorities defaulting in these important social responsibilities could be sanctioned by the only method that is fully effective; by means of the purse-strings.

The proportion of local authority borrowing raised from the government fell rapidly to 22% in 1956 and in the 1960s was less than 10%. Local authorities have moved overwhelmingly to the commercial money market to find their money and they have naturally had to pay the full rate of interest for it. Over 60% of local authority borrowing now comes from this source (and over 80% of GLC borrowing for 1974–5; see Chapter 3). There are a number of important implications. Clearly the power of central government to influence spending patterns is diminished. Moreover, the private capital market is not going to be enthusiastic to lend for purposes such as the acquisition of development land by local authorities or for large-scale public housing projects. Such activity is obviously, to a greater or lesser extent, in competition with the privately owned development system and with the concept of private landownership. In the continual and inherent conflict between private and public agencies in the field of development, finance capital knows which side its bread is buttered and, other things being equal, it will favour authorities that are known to sympathize with private development interests rather than authorities of the complexion of Clay Cross.

In view of this it will be a difficult task to achieve a more socially responsible development pattern; especially since the pension and insurance rights of millions of people are locked into the financial institutions. Ways will have to be found of underwriting these rights if profits from property development are to be affected. Thus a package of measures will be required to overcome the obstacle of the primarily private financing of new development and redevelopment.

Strategies for Change

Given the realities of politics, it is improbable that arguments based purely on the notion of social justice are likely to achieve far-reaching changes either in attitudes or in the criteria by which redevelopment decisions are made. Politicians often talk about deprivation and social injustice, especially at election time, but their decision-making tends to be dominated by two considerations; getting noisy and troublesome pressure groups off their backs and keeping down the level of the rates, or, in the case of national politics, the taxes. If this is so, it is obvious that those seeking to bring about radical change should do two things; they should exert all possible pressure on the appropriate politicians and they should base arguments largely on the sort of financial considerations that, in many cases, define the limits of a politician's understanding of the urban system he is legislating for.

The latter is really not too difficult. Housing waiting lists of 9,300 (Southwark) and 2,400 (Brighton and Hove) are not simply interesting pieces of information or even just useful comparative indices. They mean personal tragedy, family break-up, increased truancy, child-battering, psychological and physical illness and, occasionally, suicide. The causes of the disillusion and despair that produce these things are many and varied. But one cause, in many, if not in most cases, is the inability to find decent, secure and adequately sized accommodation for the household at a price it can afford. There must be thousands of families in the case-study areas whose ability to participate socially and economically in society, and whose attitude to life is determined primarily by the seriousness of their housing situation.

These families are, to use for a moment the only terms some politicians respond to, a drag on the economy both locally and nationally. They consume a disproportionate share of social services, health, welfare and educational counselling expenditure; they tend sometimes to get involved in well-supported squatting campaigns which are embarrassing and expensive to deal with and, from the point of view of national manpower needs, they are less likely to provide healthy, stable and hard-working labour. While most local authorities, and the nation as a whole, can make a reasonable estimate of the cost of solving the housing crisis it appears that little, if any, research has been done on the cost of *not* solving it. Yet on all common-sense grounds this cost must be enormous. Figures quoted in the chapter on Brighton indicate that, in this authority, expenditure *from the rates* on housing is a minute proportion of that on health, education and social services. It is certainly no part of our case to argue for cuts in these services but it does seem evident that an increased expenditure on housing, and a relatively modest one in terms of the total sums spent by local authorities, would greatly reduce the burden on the departments that currently spend so much time and energy on picking up the pieces. As in the human body, so in the urban system: prevention is better than cure.

There is another effect imposed by the housing crisis which has the degree of 'visibility' that allows it to be a factor in decision-making as opposed to simply a piece of political rhetoric. This is the relationship between the local cost of housing and the local cost and availability of labour. Some employers, with a predominantly middle-to-high-income staff, will be in favour of local 'gentrification' and expensive residential re-developments because they create a pool of executive housing in an area where it did not previously exist. But it seems likely that a majority of employers, whether of office or industrial workers, will be seeking to pay middle to low wages if possible, especially if they employ a high proportion of women. Housing costs may therefore pose a recruitment problem. It is difficult to attract labour for £30 or £35 per week when there is little or no chance of a council house and when local rents in the private sector are £15 to £20 per week for a family-sized flat. Local employers in low-paying industries understand this argument because it means either that they suffer increased labour costs by having to pay wages that enable employees to live in the area, or they suffer from labour shortage and rapid staff turnover. Since many local councillors are themselves employers, or are very sensitive to the business lobby, and since the local authority is itself one of the major employers (and one of the worst payers) in the area, we might expect some action on housing to stem from this worsening labour situation.

Conclusions

The urban conflict

The main conclusion to be drawn from this critique is that the city is a zone of conflict between competing claims for land, investment and construction resources. The advocates of a large-scale development (such as an office complex, a hotel or a marina) may claim that it will 'benefit the area as a whole' or that it will 'bring trade to the area'. We believe that the first claim is in all cases spurious and that the second expresses a sectional interest. *All* such developments benefit some (usually the business community) and penalize others (usually low-income residents). The same logic applies in reverse; to build only low-cost housing rather than offices, hotels and marinas would benefit some people (the homeless) and penalize others (the businessmen). There can be no planning decision that provides *only* benefits and, moreover, provides them in equal proportions to all residents affected.

The claim is made, both in Southwark and Brighton, that large-scale office developments will produce the rate revenue which will enable the authority to pay for housing and other necessary services so that everyone will benefit. But this depends on the use to which the increased revenue is put. In Southwark the housing crisis is getting steadily worse and in Brighton the period which saw an increase in office space by well over a third also saw an increase in the housing waiting list by a similar proportion. So office building has had sectional, rather than general, benefits for these areas. It follows from this that land-use planning is about conflict in the use of resources.

The conflict can be variously described. It is between the property owners and the property users; between the gainers and the losers; between those who need housing and those who produce offices, hotels and marinas; between finance capital and the people. The conflict was identified over a century ago by Marx and Engels as one of the basic contradictions of capitalism and it was neatly summed up by the Chairman of the LCC's

159

Housing of the Working Classes Committee late in the nineteenth century when he wrote:

The Housing problem indeed may be said to be the sum and total of all the social and economic problems that await solution . . . it provokes the vexed question of the relation between rent and wages, which easily slides into that of capital and labour. (Source: Harloe *et al.*)

Why is it that the chairmen of city housing committees do not speak in these forthright terms today although the same housing problem is still with us? How is it that the conflict has been watered down into a discussion about how the public can best 'participate' in planning? Why have we lost ground in our understanding of the fundamentals?

The answer surely lies in the various ways in which the conflict has been obscured and defused since the beginning of the century. The conflict has been *obscured* by the following means:
(i) The planning emphasis has always been laid on the visual appearance of proposed office developments, hotels or motorways. This effectively draws attention away from the underlying issue which is whether such developments have a social priority and whether they should be built at all.
(ii) Heavy stress has been given to the problem of regional inequalities and of deprivation in certain 'peripheral' areas of the country. This has drawn attention away from the reality which is that inequalities within, say, Brighton, or Southwark are as extreme as inequalities between regions. As we have seen, there is plenty of deprivation in the affluent south-east.
(iii) Research which has reached conclusions highly critical of the capitalist property development system and which has clearly identified the basic conflict has been subject to attempts at censorship by the commissioning body. This applies to the work of Williams and Anderson on Westminster and to an unknown number of other urban research projects.
(iv) Proceedings at public inquiries have served partly to obscure the conflict. For example, at the Brighton Marina inquiry the main issues were outside the terms of reference and the debate was conducted largely by legal experts using technico-legal jargon. The central issue, which was whether the proposed de-

velopment was a socially justifiable use of resources, was never properly discussed.

(v) The organization of housing has become so complex, with the profusion of subsidies, rent acts, tax concessions, voluntary agencies and divided responsibility that it is now quite difficult to determine what should be done in the short term to increase the supply of low-cost housing. Such confusion serves to obscure the basic contradiction which is that measures which benefit the landlord penalise the tenant, and vice versa.

(vi) The insurance companies, banks and pension funds which finance redevelopment are, in most people's minds, respectable and socially responsible institutions which provide protective benefits in times of personal crisis or need. Their role as investors is little known. Those facing early retirement or the loss of a job or home due to redevelopment may not realize that their problems could stem from the actions of the very institution to which they now turn for help.

The conflict has been *defused* by the following means:

(i) All planning issues are submitted to legally prescribed, but often spurious, participation procedures. These procedures may satisfy the minister but very often they fail to satisfy local residents. Nevertheless it can always be held, as long as the law is observed, that participation has occurred.

(ii) Successive governments have set up urban programmes which include such measures as Housing Action Areas, Educational Priority Areas and Community Development Projects. The total resource input into these projects has been derisory in the face of the problems and as soon as they begin to pose a radical threat to the system official support is withdrawn (see, for example, issue 15 of *West Midlands Grass Roots* for an account of the likely fate of the CDPs).

(iii) Housing authorities operate a queue system in the form of the waiting list. As Lambert and others have pointed out, the British are good at queuing and they instinctively wait patiently, accepting the 'fairness' of the principles involved. This tends to legitimize the situation and to defuse the main issue. Why does there have to be a waiting list at all? What processes produce the scarcity that necessitates a queue?

(iv) The property lobby has, on occasion, defused the situation by means of a war of attrition. They have engineered a series of inquiries by submittting a series of proposals step by step for what is, in effect, one big scheme. Local action groups might then be worn down and impoverished by having to fight a long drawn out series of battles. Alternatively the essential nature of the scheme may be concealed in order to obtain agreement in principle to the project.

All this has served to divert attention from the main point which is that the process of adding to the built environment is too vital a matter to be left in the hands of predominantly commercial interests subject only to the present unreliable and often counter-productive means of public intervention and control. The same kind of statement has been made over the past hundred years or so in relation both to education and to health and social security. The systems for the provision of these basic necessities to civilized life are now largely socialized. The system for the provision of a right balance of new buildings, houses, schools, offices, hospitals, factories, shops and so on, is no less crucial to our well-being. It, too, must come under much greater public scrutiny and accountability.

Chapter 7 What Should be Done?

We have now come to the most difficult and controversial task of all which is to put forward proposals to resolve the far-reaching issues that have been raised about the redevelopment system. Though some of the proposals are more fundamental than others, all are important and must be considered together. There is no value in continuing the division between planning solutions, economic solutions, and other groupings since redevelopment straddles all these fields and it is counter-productive to think, for example, that changes in planning law alone are sufficient to deal with the problem or that the introduction of yet another tax on development gains is the answer.

There are many politicians and civil servants who would like to believe that the undisputed problems caused by the redevelopment system can, and indeed ought, to be sorted out by tinkering with existing legislation – tightening up on loopholes in the development control system, introducing new and more subtle taxes or playing around with Office Development Permits and Industrial Development Certificates. These types of solutions have failed in the past and they will fail again. In many cases, such interventions have made things worse. Much more fundamental solutions are necessary.

The first step must be to restructure finance capital and the market in land and property to which it is tied. This process must begin with the dissolution of the property market. We have seen that the pattern of redevelopment and dereliction throughout the country is largely due to the response of the property market to the supply and demand for property and land. These forces also regulate the price of property and levels of rent and determine whether it is more profitable to build offices or housing, marinas or factories. Thus, at the heart of the redevelopment system lie the simple economics of supply and demand and unless this situation is radically altered, the redevelopment system will continue, not always perhaps in the form of a property boom but nevertheless always benefiting a small and wealthy minority.

The business world has a ready justification for this state of affairs. It argues that what is good for business is good for the community, and more particularly, that the redevelopment system provides buildings in the right place at the right price for industry. In other words, the property market is an efficient sector of the economy and should be left alone. But all the evidence we have refutes this. Development is poured into areas which are already congested, perfectly sound properties are redeveloped, land is held for investment and speculative purposes, marinas are built when there is a desperate need for housing, offices are built on the continent when new factories are needed in depressed regions of the UK. Development decisions are taken without reference to any overall economic or social plan. In some cases, huge amounts of money are spent in property dealings which do not produce any development at all, as, for example, when finance capital gambles on the 'hope' value of development sites such as Hays Wharf years before any decision to redevelop has been taken.

Our most basic proposal is that the development system be disentangled from finance capital and taken over by the state. The objective is to replace a property and planning system which responds to supply and demand with a development process which is organized around social needs and priorities. In order for this to come about, we must reverse the steady withdrawal of the state from the property system. All the key factors of production in the development process, land and buildings, development and building industries, and the institutions of finance capital, must pass into the hands of the state. Anything less than this will put beyond our reach the key social priorities of housing the homeless, providing industrial, office, and shopping units in the right locations, building community facilities, and creating a positive and socially accountable planning system.

We therefore make the following specific proposals:

1. *Draw up a National Building Plan.* The first stage in the process of public control must be the preparation of a plan which

identifies development needs in different parts of the country and estimates the number of housing units, factories, shops, offices and community facilities that are required. The exact quotas will depend upon national economic planning strategy and regional policies as well as upon the resources available. The aim of the plan will be to use building and redevelopment resources to meet regional needs. There is little point in having such a plan if it simply follows market trends such as more offices in south coast towns because that is where firms want to move to or fewer industrial premises in Inner London or the Durham Coalfield because industrial firms do not want to be located there. Development must take place where it is needed and when it is needed. In other words, instead of development following the market demand for property it will become part of the planning of local and regional economics. Previous attempts at planned building programmes such as the new towns or the efforts of local authorities such as Bermondsey in the 1930s have pointed the way by providing a vast amount of well-planned housing and community facilities where and when they were needed.

2. *Establish Public Development Corporations.* The National Building Plan will suffer the same fate as the abortive Labour Party National Plan of the 1960s unless there are publicly owned development and building agencies which have sufficient powers and resources to implement the plan. Development powers cannot continue to remain with the private property industry because property and building companies establish their priorities on the basis of profitability, not social necessity. Even if a private company were prepared to make a financial sacrifice it is impossible to imagine that private finance could be found for it. Thus public subsidies would be necessary in any case. It is, therefore, much more sensible to spend public money in a planned and accountable way by establishing public development corporations controlled from central government but perhaps organized on a regional basis. Again, the new towns have experimented with public corporations and though they have not always been as democratic and enlightened as they should have been, the potential is obvious.

3. *Take Control of the Financial Institutions.* Such sweeping

proposals as we have put forward immediately prompt the questions how much will it cost, and who is going to pay for it? In considering the actual sum, we should take into account the huge and unaccountable wastage in the present system, not to mention the economic and social benefits of producing more housing and needed facilities. In November 1974 the banking sector had £4,400 million loaned out to property, £2,700 million from the clearing banks and £1,700 million from the fringe banks, and most of this was locked into office developments, private housing, and land banks. Thus, there is no shortage of funds to invest but there is a critical need to redirect these funds away from wasteful property ventures.

Doubtless, any policy of restricting investment patterns will meet with very strong resistance from finance capital. The institutions will protest that restrictions reduce flexibility and without flexibility the entire financial system is threatened. But we might well ask whether that matters. First of all, finance capital is concerned with offering competitive terms to foreign and domestic investors. With the exception of the Bank of England, pension funds, and charitable trusts, most financial institutions are private companies with their own shareholders and profit-making imperatives. These companies are in fierce competition with each other. In fact, this competition was one of the contributory causes of the disastrous financial and property boom of 1971–3 in which many companies were offering outrageous terms to depositors which could only be met by highly speculative investment policies. The only conceivable justification for this type of competition is that the customer benefits from higher returns on his investments and higher bonuses or with-profits policies. There is no attempt at justification in terms of where the money is invested or what effect this has.

The second function of finance capital is to protect the value of funds from the ravages of inflation. Protection against inflation was achieved in the past by investing in shares or property but nowadays, with inflation approaching 25%, a more sophisticated strategy is called for. Money must be moved around more and more quickly so that an increasing percentage of the portfolio of financial companies is taken up with short-term investments.

One of the principal contradictions of these activities is that finance capital contributes to inflation and under-investment in the economy. This fact was spelled out by Mr Wedgwood Benn, Secretary of State for Industry, during an interview for the *Investors Chronicle* (6 December 1974):

> What does it really profit a fund if it puts its money into something advantageous for the short-term but contributes in that process to the denial of investment that British industry needs, so that the whole fund operates in a country which is going downhill.

The answer given by financial institutions to this charge is that it is not up to finance capital to initiate new investment strategies, but up to the government to make alternative investment profitable. In other words, unless the return on, say, industry or housing is competitive, finance capital will not invest in them.

Awareness of this situation is growing and the real controversy revolves around what steps should be taken and whether any political party or government would have the courage to do whatever is necessary. Many would argue that the services provided by finance capital such as banking, insurance, and private pensions should be provided by the state anyway and, thus a huge amount of investment power would be taken out of private hands. We believe this to be essential in the long run but consider that several major changes can be introduced in the meantime.

One possibility is that pension funds and insurance companies place with the government all contributions and premiums in excess of that needed to cover the payments they have to make each year. Thus all the excess incoming of pension funds and insurance companies which are presently used to maximize private profit could be channelled into socially useful investments by the government. As an adjunct to this policy, the state would guarantee that private pensions were indexed to inflation at the same rate as state pensions.

However, public control of finance capital must go further than this. We have seen that the institutions have accumulated vast assets in the form of stocks, shares, and property which are supposed to act as security for bank deposits, insurance policies and the like. The maintenance of the value of these assets is a major function of the finance world and leads to the situation in which finance capital puts its weight behind the lobby to protect asset values irrespective of their social value. All the assets of the institutions should therefore be transferred to the state. In the end, the institutions would have no possessions of their own and would provide financial advice and services only.

It hardly needs to be said that the finance sector would prefer to see investment controls introduced, if at all, on a voluntary basis. Some moves in this direction have been made but the limitations are readily apparent. The City Capital Markets Committee, a group of representatives of the largest institutions, made a special study of investment in industry in 1974 and concluded, not surprisingly, that a system operated by the banks and institutions would be more acceptable than a government-run scheme. Yet the Committee conceded that funds will not invest in firms or projects unless there are good prospects of making a profit, and, in a letter to *The Times* (26 November 1974) the Chairman of the Committee said that 'the provision of capital is no remedy to the problems of companies that do not make a profit'.

Nevertheless, a voluntary scheme based upon these principles was initiated by the Labour government in 1974. The Bank of England asked the financial institutions to lend a total of £1,000 million to a privately run investment bank called Finance for Industry, which was partly owned by the Bank of England. Finance for Industry made this money available for industrial firms which came to it seeking help. It was left to Finance for Industry to decide which firms were worthy of support but in general finance was not given to firms which could not be expected to make a reasonable profit and thus repay the loan. Under these circumstances, there was no risk attached to the financial sector from participation in this scheme, and moreover the Bank of England was the ultimate guarantor of all money lent to Finance for Industry.

The limitations of this sort of scheme are so obvious that the Labour government has proposed establishing a National Enterprise Board which will finance firms on a more generous and socially relevant basis than Finance for Industry. However, funds for the Board will be limited and there will be enormous pressure from the finance sector to give preference to profitable schemes.

It is equally important that finance for development is not provided on a profitability basis. The regional development corporations suggested earlier will need finance for dozens of non-profit-making projects including roads, parks, and housing. These will never be built if finance capital controls the purse strings and demands to be paid back with interest at the market rate.

4. *Take All Land and Property into Public Ownership*. It is essential to take all land and buildings into public ownership. Without this there can be no real planning of development. Significantly, the most sweeping reform of the planning system following the property boom was a proposal by the Labour Party, with sympathetic support from the Liberals, to take development land into public ownership.

Are the Labour Party's proposals really radical or well-thought-out measures? The Community Land Bill introduced in 1975 will impose a duty on local authorities to acquire land needed for development ten years ahead with compensation to existing land owners being at use value only. Since this may take some time to organize there will be a transition period in which local authorities are under no obligation to do this. Also, land held by developers at the time of publication of the *Land* White Paper in 1974 cannot be bought at use value but at a price nearer the market value. This is clearly to prevent the collapse of property companies and financial institutions which bought land at high prices and have nothing to show for it. Local authorities as land owners will be able to enter into development schemes with developers rather as they have done in the various town centre schemes referred to in Chapter 3. The idea behind it all is to involve local authorities in the land market so that they, and not just developers and land owners, benefit from the profitability of commercial development.

It has been estimated that local authorities and central government could share profits of £750 million a year when the proposals are fully implemented. But the price to be paid for this profit-making is that in every other respect the commercial property market will be unchanged. Commercial rents will rise to market levels, the rents of existing buildings will continue to flow to a select few, and as before, buildings can be traded as a commodity. In other words, the principal elements of private wealth creation will flourish and to some extent the risk of financing development schemes will be reduced. With local authorities having a financial stake in development, profits may be more reliable.

It is possible that the Community Land Bill will, like the Brown Ban on offices in London, spark off a new property bonanza. Already some developers are saying that the Bill could become a 'property man's charter' because it may decrease the supply of development sites (due to lack of local authority staff) thus causing rents to rise.

Will the Land Bill confer any benefits at all on the public? Local authorities will certainly be able to assemble land and take a more positive role in planning, but this will all cost money. Though no one knows exactly how use value will be defined, it is certain that the use value of sites in the centre of towns and cities will be high. The more it costs the more likely it will be that the poorer local authorities will go into partnership with developers for the most profitable developments. Thus, it is unlikely that hard-pressed London boroughs will buy inner urban land for new housing, open space, or industrial development, but rather will encourage a developer to build typical 'central area uses' on publicly owned land. Consequently, planning benefits may be limited to suburban areas where local authorities can buy land for housing at a large discount on the market price, while the benefits to inner urban areas which have the greatest social problems and have suffered most from redevelopment may be very small. In fact, it is quite possible that suburban Tory boroughs and county councils may gain more than the inner urban Labour boroughs.

Whether or not the Community Land Bill achieves its limited objectives, a more comprehensive public ownership scheme will be necessary if development is to be determined by social rather than market values. Not only development land but all land and buildings should revert to the state. Only in this way can planners have an adequate choice of locations for all forms of development. The existing situation, and the one which will persist under the Land Bill, is that the distribution, character and price of land uses are determined by the market. Local authorities cannot be truly positive planners until they can initiate development without reference to the economic imperatives of the market. In addition, they cannot be effective negative planners unless they own all buildings. Only in this way can they prevent gentrification, and the loss of shops, industries, and community facilities.

5. *Restructure the Basis of Commercial Rents.* We have implied throughout this book that setting commercial rents by supply and demand in the market and the receipt of these rents by private individuals and companies is undesirable. There is no hope of creating a new kind of development system or even of reforming the present one without establishing an alternative basis for setting rents. Rents in the property system perform a variety of necessary functions; they provide income and cash flow, they act as a base for calculating the value of buildings, and they are an index of supply and demand. Rental growth is essential for a flourishing property market and without it there would be no property investment nor means by which property could act as a hedge against inflation. This is why a prolonged rent freeze on all properties is an extremely serious matter to the property industry and finance capital. It is no surprise therefore, that the Bank of England and the clearing banks exerted pressure on the Labour government during 1974 to lift the freeze on commercial rents imposed by the Conservative government. The banks feared that a continuation of the rent freeze would cause a collapse of the entire banking system and inevitably the Wilson government, anxious to prevent any further loss of confidence in an evidently ailing economy and having no alternatives in mind, succumbed. Immediately after the freeze was lifted, property shares showed a sharp revival, all because the end of the freeze meant an extra £20 million in rents in 1975 alone for the top forty-five property companies.

The present rental system is extremely complex. Very few rents reflect current market levels because of the large number of irregularities caused by special leasehold arrangements and rent reviews. Rent reviews at frequent intervals are commonplace for new leases and properties and act as guarantees that rents and values will rise. But the majority of commercial tenants are paying what the property industry calls subsidized rents, or rents which were set some while ago and are below market levels.

Thus, the users of property stand to suffer considerably when rents become established at market levels. It is noteworthy that when the government announced the end of the rent freeze many industrialists and small businesses were extremely angry. It was a case of finance capital prevailing over other sections of the business world.

What form could an alternative rental system take? One suggestion that has been put forward to alleviate the worst hardship is the establishment of a rent subsidy for businesses. It is argued that the flight of small shops and businesses from cities could be stemmed with selective subsidies in much the same way as various subsidies are employed to attract industry to depressed areas of the country. But the difficulty with a subsidy system is that it could easily become unfair or end up subsidizing essential services which were already profitable. For example, if it was agreed to subsidize pharmacists in inner urban areas, then the giant Boots company would take a large share of the total subsidy. Subsidies may be better than nothing but we consider this approach to be partial and inferior to restructuring the entire basis of commercial rents.

Another possible alternative is to introduce the idea of a fair rent for commercial property similar to that introduced for residential property under the 1965 Rent Act. Under this legislation, application for a fair rent to be determined could be made by either landlord or tenant or both to the council Rent Officer. The Rent Officer then had to assess rents on the basis of comparable properties in the locality of the property in question. All elements of scarcity were to be ignored by the Rent Officer. The result of this assessment procedure was that the rent increases proposed by landlords were moderated to some extent, although in other respects market differentials were built in. For example, identical properties in, say, Newcastle or Inner London were assessed at different levels because the comparable properties chosen in each case were those in the immediate locality. Moreover, since the Rent Act stated that rents fixed by Rent Officers should be fair to landlord and fair to tenant the profit-making imperatives of private landlords were inevitably taken into consideration. For these reasons, other alternatives must be sought.

A really radical alternative would have to make a clean break with past legislation. Commercial rents are at present made up of the following components: the effects of supply and demand or scarcity, the effects of land values or location, the landlord's profit, and lastly the costs of erecting and maintaining the building. We propose a rent system which takes into account *only* the last component. This value could be calculated by valuers from local authorities and central government and the rent which a tenant would pay would be assessed by a Rent Officer on the basis of this value. There might be concessions for certain categories of use such as local government or community centre, but generally rents would reflect only the quality and age of buildings. Consequently, in contrast with the present situation, similar buildings in different locations would have the same base value for calculating rents. Local authorities would have the critical responsibility of deciding which land uses and activities should have preference in different locations. The great advantage of this type of rent setting is that it would change the emphasis of the property system from an obsession with financial values to a concern for the social value of land and buildings.

6. *Reduce the Power of the Property Professions.* Whatever changes take place in the property and planning systems the state must recognize that it is likely to be fiercely opposed by the professional bodies representing those who act on behalf of property developers and finance capital. The Royal Institution of Chartered Surveyors (RICS), the Incorporated Society of Valuers and Auctioneers (ISVA) and the accountancy professions are the most important professional groups in the field of property valuation. Their importance is that they set up the codes of practice for their professions and establish working definitions of vague though crucial terms such as 'use value', and 'fair rents', and through their members in local authorities they can influence the decisions of local authority planners and valuers.

It is, of course, of vital importance that the definition of critical concepts like use value are not left to groups like the RICS. The RICS has always stood behind the property industry and has always opposed government intervention in the property market. Their members act for landowners, developers, and local authorities and are not inclined to be very sympathetic to any proposals which attack the property industry. Moreover, they have a strong vested interest in increasing property values and expanding the private sector since generally valuation fees are proportional to the value of the property surveyed. Hence the higher the value of the property and the more frequent the valuation the better off they are. Therefore, new legislation must be accompanied by definitions and codes of practice drawn up by those who are sympathetic to the social and political objectives of the legislation.

7. *Base Planning on Compensatory Principles.* If we accept that the present effects of land use planning are, on the whole, *regressively* redistributive, and if we judge this to be undesirable, then it follows that we should attempt to bring about a planning philosophy that produces *progressive* redistribution; that benefits the poor rather than the rich. This means that major planning decisions must be approached with new questions uppermost. The main questions must be 'what are the probable wealth redistributive effects of these proposals?' and 'how will these proposals affect the lower-income groups in this area?' Once these questions have been thought out the decision must be approached in the light of the question 'which outcome will be of greatest benefit to deprived groups in the area?'

If, following careful analysis along these lines and after involving local people in the decision-making (see 11 below), it is decided that some form of disruptive redevelopment is necessary on general social grounds, then complete appraisal should be made of the costs involved for all households affected and full compensatory reimbursement should be made. It is pointless to argue that the calculations involved are too difficult. Industrial concerns and local authorities are capable of carrying out the most sophisticated cost-benefit calculations when it suits them to do so.

To approach planning and redevelopment in this way would be to align it with other major aspects of social policy aimed at redressing the worst inequalities evident in society (for example free health care, compensatory education measures, and the various benefits for low-income groups). From a social policy point of view the present system is totally illogical. The overall pattern of planning decision resulting from present practice is generating a wide range of problems for low income people. Vast sums are then spent on support services of one kind or another to try to cushion the bad effects produced by the decisions. If we take this wider view, the system makes no sense at all; it is working against itself.

8. *Make Political Appointments in the Civil Service and Local Government.* Since the planning system allocates scarce resources it is essentially political. It is axiomatic, in a democracy, that political decisions should be made by politicians (who are elected) rather than by bureaucrats (who are not). But there is much evidence to show that civil servants and local government officers are often instrumental in policy-making and are acting as non-elected political advocates. The Crossman diaries paint a picture of a situation where a minister was committed to a policy without his knowledge, where the Treasury's view of the world was allowed to dictate housing policy and where civil servants appeared to be running ministries as they wanted to. Examples were given of the 'management' of Cabinet minutes and no doubt the practice extends to lesser committees. In fact, the situation was summed up in a recent television statement by a retired head of the civil service to the effect that it did not matter too much what successive governments did since the civil service could always provide continuity and keep us on the right track.

The case-study chapters in this book have provided examples where the context for important decisions has been defined by the technical advice of the Department of the Environment and the officers of the local authorities. Such advice, which may incorporate the value system and political preferences of the adviser, can have a crucial effect on outcomes, as much by what it omits as by what it includes. In any case, and this may not be widely known, politicians sometimes have less access than officials to information. This became evident in the case of the proposed Brighton Marina late in 1974 when the leader of the Labour group on the Council was denied access to certain files on the authority's dealings with the Marina Company. Such 'confidentiality' makes a mockery of democracy and is quite unnecessary.

Apologists for the present system could argue that one is simply up against institutional size and the complexity of modern technology. They might say that the issues are so complicated that only trained and impartial experts can be trusted to advise on the decisions and that it is axiomatic that in Britain we rely not only on the expertise but also on the complete integrity of these experts. This may be generally true, but anyone watching the various performances in the Brighton issues might, by now, be feeling as highly sceptical, as most readers of the growing number of studies of the decision-making pattern in other authorities such as Croydon, Tynemouth and Newcastle upon Tyne. In any case, we have already argued that the issues are not technical problems to be arbitrated by experts, however reasonable and honest, but genuine political conflicts about resources In a democracy, the people as a whole, via their elected representatives, should have the right to decide the outcome of such conflicts.

The issue we have touched upon, the power distribution between elected members and officials, is a general one. Politicians will presumably always need a bureaucracy or at least a secretariat. Problems begin to arise when the form does not truly reflect the function. In the case of land-use planning we have argued that the bureaucracy is, in effect, making important political decisions. But the defect is that civil servants and officials do not have to reveal their politics to the electorate; indeed they are not supposed to have any, which is a patent absurdity. They do not have to argue their case with the electors, they cannot be voted out, and to protect their position they must subscribe to the myth that their advice is non-political, whether they believe it or not.

It follows that either officials should play a much reduced role in decision-making or that the most important non-elected advisers should be political appointees. The former solution, which is perhaps preferable, seems difficult to achieve except in the long term (as all who have experienced the system at close hand would probably agree). So we propose that serious attention should be given to the idea of making senior central and local government appointments on a political basis, and for the life of the government or council concerned. Then politicians could at least be sure that their policies would be implemented rather than blocked; we could all be sure that the chief executive giving evidence 'on behalf of the town' was more directly accountable to democratic mandate; and senior civil servants and officials would be less sure of their position at the top of the bureaucratic tree. In short, there would be a wide spread of benefits.

9. *Extend the Definition of 'Planning Grounds'.* At present planning discussions are carried on almost entirely in terms of 'planning grounds'. These, in turn, are defined by the planning legislation. But, as in the case of the political structures, there is a discrepancy between form and function. Many social and economic factors which are undeniably significant to the rational resolution of a planning conflict are excluded from discussion when an application is being considered either by a planning committee or at an inquiry.

This can again be illustrated by reference to the Brighton Marina inquiry which was held late in 1974. The saga of the marina is a lengthy and, in places, involved one and for present purposes we are much more concerned with the principles it illustrates than with the specific details of the case. But briefly, the 1974 development application was for a glorified offshore leisure/residential development with a luxury hotel, a wide range of mostly high cost entertainments, moorings for 2,000 or more boats (twenty-six foot long and upward) and 1,450 very high-cost flats. A development on this enormous scale would obviously have considerable planning implications. Some of these were reflected in the terms of reference for the inquiry which mentioned such aspects as the visual impact and traffic implications of the marina, and the need and justification for the proposed amounts of shopping, exhibition and residential space.

These terms of reference made sense as far as they went but at least two crucially important planning issues were not mentioned: the impact that marina employees would make on the local housing situation and the 'resource diversion' effect of committing enormous input resources to the construction of the marina. As we have seen, the local housing situation is critically bad. Adding 1,450 flats, to be sold at up to £50,000 each, will not benefit the low-cost housing sector where the problems are concentrated. But the addition of between 500 and 1,000 extra employees who will have to compete in the low cost rented sector, which the marina company's own figures seemed to imply, could only mean ever increasing housing pressures on an already over-stretched market.

One solution might have been to grant the planning consent subject to the development including sufficient low cost housing to accommodate all the lower income workers employed on the site. This course, however, appears to be impossible since conditions of this sort could be contested by the developers on the grounds that they were not planning conditions. And such is the present state of the law that this view would probably be upheld in the courts. Yet from a social planning viewpoint it is vitally necessary for the planning authority to be able to control not only the number of accommodation units on a new development but also the price range of the units.

Equally significant is the argument about the use of resources. The construction and operation of the marina would consume resources on a vast scale. These inputs would include capital, building plant and materials, labour, professional skills, and the time of local government departments. These inputs could be put to a more socially relevant use such as building low-cost housing elsewhere in the sub-region. It is well known that many local authorities experience difficulties in attracting bids for low-cost housing developments because under the present system it is obviously more attractive to developers to become involved in leisure projects such as hotels and marinas.

The Marina Action Campaign were advised by their barrister not to introduce this line of argument since it did not come under any of the terms of reference. Yet, if the economic concept of 'opportunity cost' means anything it means that resources committed to one task (the construction of a marina) cannot at the same time be used for another (say, the production of low-cost housing). The matter is one of priorities and choice, and that is what planning is supposed to be about. But this issue, perhaps, the most important one of the lot, was simply judged not to be a 'planning' matter!

10. *Adopt Socio-Economic Land-Use Categories.* At present

most 'strategic' land-use planning is seen in terms of devising land zonings, in accordance with the observed trends of population and employment change in the area. The main aim seems to be to discern trends and to plan to accommodate them. Thus, at a local planning level, once an area shows particular social or economic tendencies, the effect of zoning land for residential or industrial use will usually be to produce specific planning applications from developers which reinforce the tendencies. For example, a residential area which is already high status will tend to attract development applications for more high-status housing. Alternatively, in an inner urban redevelopment, land zoned for shops or industrial use will often produce profit maximizing developments which, almost by definition, work against the interests of local people by producing higher rents for shops and factory space than were charged in the area before redevelopment. Local authorities appear to have, or to exercise, less influence over the cost of living and the socio-economic evolution of their area than over its physical appearance. Given our present understanding of the functioning of cities this is surely a misplaced priority.

The situation could be brought under closer local authority control, regardless of what steps are taken about public land ownership, by adding a socio-economic dimension to the largely physical set of land-use categories currently used in planning. There is little chance of achieving social planning of the sensitivity required when large areas of land are zoned for residential or general business uses. A residential zoning can attract a wide variety of planning applications from developers and a planning authority aiming to encourage more low-cost housing is placed in an unnecessarily weak bargaining position. What is needed is the adoption of categories that enable the authority to control much more closely the *social* pattern of development. Categories such as low-cost housing, neighbourhood shops, low-rent industrial space, community facilities and amenities and so on would enable the planning authority to set out more accurately the pattern of social and economic development it would like to see in the area. At present a planning authority which turned down a development application for luxury private housing on the grounds that low-cost housing was needed in the area would find itself in a weak legal position at the appeal that would probably result. The developers would probably argue that as long as the use they were proposing conformed to the zoning, then an economic reason, the cost of the eventual houses, was not a planning ground and was therefore an insufficient reason for rejection.

11. *Ensure Public Involvement in Planning Decisions.* The many defects in the present procedures for involving the public in planning decisions were set out in the previous chapter and examples of some of them occurred in the case-study chapters. Present procedures used by planning authorities to sound out public opinion are primitive in the extreme. All social scientists know that public exhibitions and meetings attract a tiny biased sample of the total population, and even amateur politicians know that public meetings can easily be designed to absorb, rather than to transmit, public pressure.

Yet a great deal is known about cheap and reliable ways of assessing public opinion. Public opinion polls, government statistical departments and purveyors of new washing powders are all highly expert at gauging public responses. They achieve accurate results because it suits their interests to do so. They do not expect members of the public to make a journey to a library, inspect a document phrased in general and hypothetical terms, and then to send off written comments by post. Instead they carry out well-designed random sample surveys in order to ensure that they get a virtually complete cross section of opinion. The gulf between the state of the art of opinion sounding and the methods actually used lead one to have suspicions either about the competence of most planning authorities or about the sincerity of their intentions.

Opponents of participation have argued that public involvement causes delays, that people are apathetic towards planning and that they are interested only in issues that directly affect them and not in the wider implications. The first argument can be conceded. Delay is inevitable if proper consultation procedures are carried out. Delay means loss to developers but often it means beneficial second and third thoughts about the wisdom of a development. In any case the length of the delay seems to be roughly correlated with the opposition aroused by the proposal

(Piccadilly is a classic example) and thus it is the most contentious proposals that experience most delay – which seems a form of rough justice.

The second and third arguments are linked. Apathy probably stems from a lack of understanding of the impact of a large-scale decision on the individual. In fact, the third argument itself makes the point that where individuals *can* see the connection, perhaps because of the proximity of what is proposed, they are anything but apathetic. For example, people are interested in whether or not they have to pay an extra £5 per week rent or mortgage repayment but they may not be able to connect this increase with a planning decision taken five years previously to build, say, a marina which drastically increased the demand for, and thus the cost of, accommodation in the area. Such implications need to be clearly spelled out.

At present there is a statutory duty to publicize details of the land uses and physical appearance of a proposed development. In some ways these are matters of secondary importance. What local people really need to know is whose money is behind the project, what profit might result for the landowners, leaseholders, developers, and professional agencies, and what planning gain is being returned to the local authority. In addition, they need to know what effect the development will have on the cost and quality of living in the area. Only in these circumstances will local residents and workers be able to decide whether the balance of private and community gain is one to which they can lend their support. But the creation of a climate of public awareness in which these questions become automatic is not something that will happen overnight. It is a long-term task which must be attacked in a variety of ways.

12. *Expand Community Action.* One of the most important ways of increasing awareness of the workings of the redevelopment system and of organizing pressure on local authorities is through community action. Over the last five years, community action has provided an important political focus for many locally based groups and individuals including tenants' associations, amenity groups, and trade unionists. In many instances, community groups have been the only reliable source of information on re-

development controversies and often have been successful in delaying or modifying redevelopment schemes and plans which have threatened the community. Much has been achieved as well in raising the level awareness concerning redevelopment processes among local representatives.

There are however a number of problems involved in basing a strategy for radical change on community action. In the first place, community groups often have a parochial view since their concern is with the workings of the property system in their own area and their actions are not specifically aimed at the defects in the system as a whole. They may also be dedicated to conservation rather than restructuring the system and are quite likely to be open to cooption by local authorities. They are also likely to be transitory and to last only as long as it takes to achieve, or fail to achieve, a specific aim. Finally there is the danger that successful community resistance to redevelopment in one area will simply export the problem to some other area which is 'softer' from the developers' viewpoint. The property development industry is a many-headed monster which if frustrated in one area will turn its attention to another.

In view of these problems, can community action become an effective political movement? There are wide differences of political belief within community action. Members of different groups and even members within the same group may span the political spectrum. The all-party interest in the recent proposals to set up neighbourhood councils and the proliferation of community groups in middle- and upper-income areas are evidence that community action is by no means the preserve of those on the political left. Community groups are thus usually loose coalitions held together more by issues than ideology. Moreover, community groups generally cannot call upon the same mass support base as the trades union movement (to which community action has only loose ties), and being essentially outside the local political system may have less influence over local affairs in practice than local authority officers or ward party members. The main value of community action lies in making the rest of the local community as well as local authorities, aware of the issues. Also, because it springs from the grass roots, community action is a mine of detailed information about the locality.

The long term significance of community action can be judged more easily in terms of its impact on the organization and composition of political parties, tenants associations, and trades unions. Of particular importance is the wider use of the power of the trades unions in community action, not only in general support but also in the use of selective industrial action. At the moment practically the only links between community groups and trades unions are through local trades councils. Very few union branches are affiliated directly with community groups so that community action is usually one step removed from the grass roots of the union movement. A good example of the detachment of the unions from local redevelopment issues is the luke-warm involvement of the trades unions in the vast redevelopment plans for London's Docklands. All the Trades Union Congress has managed to do so far is to call a poorly attended conference and publish a couple of discussion papers. There have been no suggestions of actions in support of, or in opposition to particular types of schemes. Yet obviously the unions by using their industrial power could do a great deal more to influence the course of redevelopment.

13. *Increase the Involvement of Local Political Organizations.* Ward party politics, as everyone knows, are lamentably inactive in most parts of the country. In inner London, for example, membership of most political parties is falling steadily and local ward party meetings are usually less well attended than the meetings of community groups. Resolutions by local wards get lost in the party bureaucracy and few actions or support for actions stem from ward parties. More often than not the wards support the political establishment, rather than putting pressure on local councillors. The council for its part usually makes no effort to consult with local ward parties on issues which affect the ward. In Southwark, for example, no attempt is made by the council to sound out the views of the ward on local plans, redevelopment proposals, or policies that affect the livelihood of people in the area, many of whom are Labour Party voters. Quite clearly this state of affairs will have to change dramatically if the Labour Party is to introduce any effective changes in the redevelopment system. We are not suggesting that the answer lies in the election

of more enlightened or more left-wing councillors, but that local political organizations must increase their own awareness and involvement in redevelopment issues.

14. *Deal with Planning/Development in the School Curriculum.* The ability of local pressure groups to attract support probably hinges upon the extent to which the local population as a whole is alive to the issues. The aim must be to work towards a situation where the *majority* of the population in an area, and not just the informed minority, can be mobilized against the development lobby. At present the general run of school leavers is better versed in quadratic equations than local politics; more knowledgeable about the Roman occupation of Britain than about the squatters' occupation of Centre Point. Whether these emphases occur by accident or by design they do seem inappropriate, to say the least, for people who soon after leaving school will be competing in an extremely tight housing market.

Opinions may vary about the appropriate age to introduce into the curriculum such questions as 'why are some people without a home?', 'who owns the centre of our town?' or 'who decided that the marina should be built?' We feel that somewhere between the ages of twelve and fourteen might be about right. The questions are conceptually no more difficult than many others raised at that age and they are a lot more relevant to the process of becoming a questioning adult.

Material of the type covered in this book should be dealt with throughout the secondary-school curriculum. The rapidly increasing range of courses under the general heading of environmental studies, or something similar, provide an appropriate vehicle. Some material of the right kind, for example Ward and Fyson's book *Streetwork*, has already been published and local newspaper files, council documents and estate agents' windows provide free teaching resources. The laboratory of the city is readily available to the vast majority of children in our highly urbanized society. And once the basic interests of the various groups have been identified there can be few more educational experiences than watching a local council discussing a provocative planning issue. Given the relevance of the issues to everyday life, there seems to be no good reason for not giving urban planning and development a very serious place in the school curriculum.

15. *Reorganize Urban Analysis in Higher Education.* The same issues and processes should be examined in greater depth by those who go on to higher education. University and college curricula have for a long time included the disciplines of urban geography, urban planning and so on. But these courses have little cutting edge because of their misplaced emphases. Urban geographers have produced hundreds of articles on urban land use and social area analysis, central business districts, patterns of residential mobility, urban rent gradients and the like. Much of this empirical material has made the assumptions that people are in a position to *choose* their place of residence and that it is fully to be expected that sites will tend towards a 'highest and best' (that is, most profitable) use. The assumptions, in other words, have been those of capitalism and until recently few authors have questioned their applicability. Few have realized that the pattern of urban land use does not just evolve; it is carefully managed, in ways we have described, by self-interested groups whose membership can be specified and whose operations can be closely observed and analysed. Little is to be gained from mapping or modelling the end product of these processes when it is the processes themselves that need to be understood.

There are a number of reasons for this misapplication of effort. Academics tend to read each other's work rather than reading the trade journals of the development industry or the financial press. Thus so-called theories of the city (for example those of Burgess or Hoyt) achieve a status quite unrelated to their explanatory power because they are repeated from one textbook to another. Another reason is that academic study is organized in disciplines, the boundaries between which, as David Harvey has rightly remarked, are inherently counter-revolutionary. This is partly because they have a built-in tendency towards self-justification, especially when empire-building professors get to work. But more significantly it is because the most challenging of today's urban problems such as housing and the operation of the land market do not fall neatly into any discipline; they straddle several. To get to grips with them one has to leave the disciplinary framework and focus on the problem. Since few academics appear ready to do this, the people who really *do* understand how things work are mostly practitioners in the field; they are quietly making a lot of money free from such publicity as the attention of academics might produce.

Our educational prescriptions are therefore quite simple. The redevelopment process should be studied throughout the post-primary educational system. People should be encouraged to ask awkward questions about urban planning and development and should be helped to realize how relevant these questions are *to them*. They should not be fed with covertly capitalist assumptions. In higher education there is the additional problem of overcoming the reactionary effects of disciplinary boundaries. Topic-based degree courses (for example 'Urban Studies') seem to offer the best hope of doing this. If, in time, most of the population have been encouraged to think about these issues and about the nature of the capitalist land market, we feel sure that direct action will be much easier to organize and that much greater public vigilance will be exercised on the behaviour of politicians and officials.

16. *Use Research Effort More Effectively*. Much expensive research has recently been carried out on cities. The aim of a lot of it has been to assess the incidence of urban deprivation. Typically, a large number of census and other variables have been measured for various zones of the city in question. All studies have reached the predictable conclusion that things are worse in the older inner suburbs. This conclusion lost the capacity to surprise many years ago. There is no need to carry out yet more of these studies, at very considerable expense, when the general situation is clear. It may be in the interests of government, expressed via the pattern of research grants, to continue with inquiries of this kind, since research is cheaper than action. But it is time to direct a greater effort at the *causes* of the situation, not at its effects.

The inappropriateness of much centrally funded research to the basic issues may be judged from the February 1975 *Newsletter* of the Social Science Research Council. The SSRC is the main promoter of official research in the social sciences and this particular newsletter dealt with housing. It included much about systems approaches, research strategies and initiatives, programme items, and 'independent but publicly sponsored research'. But nowhere was there a mention of research into the relationships between housing scarcity and property values, between housing costs and incomes, between finance capital and the political power structure, and between urban redevelopment and wealth redistribution.

What we need is research which questions the present structure and which focuses on the operation of the system, not on its output. We have tried to identify some of the key decision-makers in the planning/development process. These include senior civil servants, investment fund managers, local government chief officers, merchant bankers and financiers, as well as developers themselves. Research is needed on the backgrounds, ideologies, values and assumptions of these people and on the patronage relationships that exist between them. We need to know from other case-study situations how these relationships operate to produce development decisions. We need to use a wide accountancy base to get an exact answer to the crucial question 'who gains and who loses?' And we need to relate all this to a general understanding of the workings of capitalism.

Postscript

Six months after giving the interview quoted on page 167, Mr Benn was moved from his post as Secretary of State for Industry to a less politically sensitive Cabinet job. A few months previously, in early 1975, Mr Crosland, as Secretary of State for the Environment, set up an Advisory Group on Commercial Property Development to help him with policy formulation. The professional affiliations of this group read like a roll call of the capitalist development system.

These events, and others, strengthen our suspicion that the property machine has nothing to fear from the present policies of the Labour government.

Bibliography

Abbey Property Fund, *Annual Report 1973*.

Alonso, W., 'A Theory of the Urban Land Market', *Papers and Proceedings of the Regional Science Association*, 6, 1960, pp. 154–9.

Amalgamated Investment and Property Co. Ltd, *Report and Accounts 1973*.

Ambrose, P. J., 'The Myth of Urban Planning', *Geographical Magazine*, October 1974.

Atkinson, A. B., *Unequal Shares*, Penguin, 1974.

Bagley, C., *et al.*, 'Social Structure and the Ecological Distribution of Mental Illness, Suicide, and Delinquency', *Psychological Medicine*, 3, 2 May 1973, pp. 177–87.

Barker, G., *et al.*, *Highrise and Superprofits*, Dumont Press Graphix, Kitchener, Ontario, 1973.

Board of Trade, Control of Office and Industrial Development Act, *Annual Reports*, 1966–1973, HMSO.

Borough of Brighton, *Jubilee Street, Church Street Redevelopment Area*, Officers Report, August 1974.

Borough of Hove, *44th Annual Report of the Director of Housing 1972*.

Burgess, E. W., 'The Growth of the City', in Park, R. E. *et al.*, *The City*, Chicago, 1925.

Centre for Advanced Land Use Studies, *Investment in Property*, College of Estate Management, University of Reading, 1974.

Colenutt, B. and McFadden, W., 'The Property Lobby', *Street Research*, no. 4, 1974.

Community Planning Associates, *West Midlands Grass Rooots*, Finch Road, Lozells, Birmingham.

Community Action Investigator's Handbook, PO Box 665, London SWI, 1975.

Counter Information Services, *The Recurrent Crisis of London*, 1973; *Your Money and Your Life*, 1974.

County and District Properties Ltd, *Report and Accounts*, 1973.

County Borough of Brighton, *Jubilee Street Development, Developers Brief*, 1973; *Council Agenda*, November 1973; *Greater Brighton Structure Plan*, 1974.

Crawford, K., 'Both Eyes on Government', *Investors Chronicle*, 16 November 1973.

Croydon Suburban Press, *The Democratic Charade Exposed*, 433 London Road, Croydon.

Daniel, W. W., 'What Ever Happened to the Workers in Woolwich?', *Political and Economic Planning*, 1972.

Day, A., 'The Nation's Wealth – Who Owns it?', *Observer*, 20 January 1974.

Dearlove, J., *The Politics of Policy in Local Government*, Cambridge University Press, 1973.

Department of the Environment, *Housing and Construction Statistics*, HMSO, annual; *Strategic Plan for the South East*, HMSO, 1970; *Local Authority/Private Enterprise Partnership Schemes*, HMSO, 1972; *Land*, Cmnd. 5730, HMSO, 1974; *Review of the Development Control System, Final Report*, Dobry, G., HMSO, 1975.

Department of Trade and Industry, *Business Monitor Quarterly Statistics*, HMSO.

Engels, F., *The Housing Question*, Progress Publishers, Moscow, 1970.

Fleming, J. S. and Little, I. M., *Why We Need a Wealth Tax*, Methuen, 1974.

Galvin, P., 'Hidden Gold', *Estates Gazette*, 217, 1971, pp. 1215–17.

Gans, H. J., *People and Plans*, Penguin, 1972.

Glennester, H., 'Education and Inequality', in P. Townsend and N. Bosanquet (eds.), *Labour and Inequality*, Fabian Society, 1972.

Glyn, A. and Sutcliffe, B., *British Capitalism, Workers and the Profits Squeeze*, Penguin, 1972.

Government Statistical Service, *Social Trends*, no. 5, HMSO, 1974.

Greater London Council, *Greater London Development Plan – Written Statement*, 1971.

Hambro Property Fund, *Annual Report 1973*.

Hardman, H., *The Dispersal of Government Workers from London*, Cmnd 5322, HMSO, 1973.

Harloe, M., *et al.*, *The Organisation of Housing*, Heinemann, 1974.

Harvey, D., *Social Justice and the City*, Edward Arnold, 1973.

Institute for Economic Affairs, *Government and the Land*, Institute for Economic Affairs Readings, 13, 1974.

Kincaid, J. C., *Poverty and Inequality in Britain*, Penguin, 1973.

Lambert, J., *et al.*, *Neighbourhood Politics and Housing Opportunities*, paper given at the Environmental Studies Conference at York University, January 1975.

Lionel, R., and Partners, *Central London Office Premises Report 1973*.

Lipsey, D., *Labour and Land*, Fabian Society, 1973.

Marriott, O., *The Property Boom*, Pan, 1969.

Marx, K., *Capital*, vol. 1, Moscow, 1954; *The Economic and Philosophic Manuscripts of 1844*, International Publishers, 1964.

Merton, R. K., *Social Theory and Social Structure*, Free Press, 1968.

Miliband, R., *The State in Capitalist Society*, Quartet, 1973.

Mineworkers Staff Pension Fund, *Annual Report 1973*.

North Southwark Community Development Group, *The Property Market and the Redevelopment of North Southwark*, December 1973.

Page, H., *Report of the Committee to Review National Savings*, Cmnd 5273, HMSO, 1973.

Post Office Staff Superannuation Fund, *Annual Report 1973*.

Property Growth Assurance Company, *Annual Report 1973*.

Quilter, Hilton, Goodison and Co., *Property 1974*; *Property 1975*.

Revell, J. R. S., 'Changes in the Social Distribution of Poverty in Britain during the Twentieth Century', *Actes du troisième congrès international d'histoire économique*, Munich, 1965.

Roe, A., *The Financial Independence of the Economy 1957–1961*, Chapman & Hall, 1971.

Shelter, *Face the Facts*, 1969.

Southwark, London Borough of, *Southwark's Thames-side – A Strategy Plan, 1973*.

Spiegelberg, R., *The City*, Quartet, 1973.

St Martins Property Corporation Ltd, *Report and Accounts 1973*.

Walton, J., 'London – The World's Shopping Centre', *Investors Chronicle*, 16 November 1973.

Ward, C., and Fyson, A., *Streetwork*, Routledge, 1973.

Williams, J., and Anderson, J., *Planning in Central London: Research and Censorship*, mimeographed, 1972.

Young, M., and Willmott, P., *Family and Kinship in East London*, Penguin, 1972.